THIS BOOK
BELONGS TO
Nicola Foss
BINGO

The School at Schellebelle

Gertie Evenhuis

The School at Schellebelle

Translated from the
Dutch by Lance Salway
Illustrated by
Rien Poortvliet

Kestrel Books

KESTREL BOOKS
Published by Penguin Books Ltd
Harmondsworth, Middlesex, England

First published in Great Britain 1975
Originally published in the Netherlands by Van Goor Zonen Den Haag, 1964 under the title *De School van Schellebelle*

ISBN 0 7226 5222 4
Printed in Great Britain by
Ebenezer Baylis and Son Ltd
The Trinity Press,
Worcester and London

Contents

1. The year begins

It was the last night of the year, at exactly twelve o'clock, and the bell was ringing loudly in the tower of an old church in the south of Holland.

A boy was pulling the bell rope. His name was Andreas, and he was eleven years old. There's nothing very special about that, of course, for there are plenty of eleven-year-old boys about. But it was the first time that Andreas had been allowed to ring the bell, and that *was* special. It was dark, and he could hear above his head the mysterious noises that can only be heard in an old tower: the creaking of ancient beams, the squeaking and fluttering of unseen creatures, and, over them all, the mighty boom of the bell.

Gasping with effort, Andreas let his body rise with the rope and then fall back again. His father was listening outside, and the teacher too. Inside, behind him, stood the old verger. Andreas would rather have died than lose control of the bell rope in their presence. If he grasped it too high, he would be dragged up into the air. Ringing a bell isn't all that easy and it's not surprising that the verger watched him suspiciously.

Andreas pulled the rope again and the heavy chimes of the bell drifted over the wide, flat countryside. The new year had begun.

Andreas had a friend, called Frank Camillemans. He was a tall, quiet boy with freckles. His hair was brown, unlike Andreas' own untidy fair hair. Frank was good at running. And his father owned at least twenty horses. Now the two boys followed their fathers out of the village of Klaaskinderkerke along the road to Schellebelle, where they lived. The teacher rode home, too, through the crowds who were welcoming the new year in the streets. When the verger had closed the heavy oak doors of the church, Andreas had heard him shout: 'Happy New Year! And good luck with the school!' The teacher disappeared past them now on his moped.

The two boys walked behind their fathers along the dike which led to the village of Schellebelle. They were both panting a little because their fathers' legs were so much longer than their own.

'Of course I'm coming with you,' Andreas' father had said. 'But on foot. I'm always glued to my tractor. Or the car. And it's hard to tell where *you* begin and your bike ends! It'll be nice to walk home to our farm in the moonlight. Just like old times.'

And so Andreas' mother and his sisters Francine and Sara had driven home in the car, while Andreas and Frank walked back with their fathers.

The village lay behind them now. High in the freezing sky, the stars and the moon shone down on the road and on the dunes.

'How's it going, men?' Frank's father called back to them. The boys could see a little cloud of breath rising from his mouth. They grumbled happily back. Their fathers' conversation drifted towards them as they walked.

' . . . more and more families are leaving for the city. And there's nothing one can do about that . . . '

'There aren't as many horses about as there used to be,' said Frank's father thoughtfully.

'If only Polderman hadn't taken his five boys

from the school,' Andreas' father went on bitterly. 'And all because of that stupid quarrel. It said in the letter that . . . '

Their voices were lowered now and the boys couldn't hear what the letter had said. Only by listening carefully could they make out a few scraps of conversation:

' . . . I have to admit, the lane's in a dreadful state . . . '

' . . . I wouldn't take *my* children . . . '

And then, 'He said that he's had enough. And now no one can get past at all. Now, what *I* say is . . . '

Suddenly the silence on the dike was shattered by distant factory whistles and ships' sirens. They could hear, too, the foghorns that lay to the north in the mouth of the River Schelde.

'Are you looking forward to going back to school?' Andreas asked.

Frank shrugged his shoulders in the darkness. 'Yes,' he said. 'Well, it all depends.' He stopped for a moment to test a frozen puddle with his heel. 'If you ask me, it won't be up to much. With all the little children coming into our class.' The boys ran to catch up with the two shadows ahead of them. Frank went on, 'Of course, Ghislain and Sara think it's marvellous.'

Andreas sniffed loudly. It was only to be expected that the small children would be delighted that

Miss Jonathan had to leave the school. Not that they had anything against her. On the contrary, they were very fond of her. But it was boring having a lady teacher all the time. Especially when they were almost as big as the older children.

'They just want to be with the big ones,' said Andreas scornfully.

The big ones. Andreas and Frank and their friends were the big ones. They sat in the other classroom and their teacher was a man.

But now I must tell you a little about the place where the children live.

Where Holland ends and Belgium begins lies Zeeland. There, day and night, you can hear the droning of the wild grey River Schelde that runs, broad and dangerous, into the sea. When there is mist, the whistles of the big ships on their way to Antwerp wail over the land and over the water. There are dunes along the coast. Behind them lie wide polders – fields that are lower than the sea – and these are separated by dikes. There are farms on the polders, and churches, and villages. One of the villages is Schellebelle. It's much smaller than a village, really, for less than two hundred people live there. It isn't even big enough to have its own church. The nearest church is in Klaaskinderkerke and you can see the tower clearly from Schellebelle. But there is a school there. There are only thirty-one children, but at least it is a school. There is a schoolmaster for the older children and a mistress, Miss Jonathan, for the younger ones. At least, there *were* two teachers in the school at Schellebelle. If the number of children in a village school fell below thirty-one, then the school could only have one teacher. And this is what had happened at Schellebelle. Mr Polderman had taken his five sons away from the school and so, because there were now only twenty-six children left, Miss Jonathan had been forced to leave. The schoolmaster, who usually taught only the older children, would now have to teach all the children by himself.

None of the children really knew why Mr Polderman had taken his sons away. All they knew was that there had been a quarrel and that, because of this, the Polderman boys weren't coming back to the school. The one thing they *were* sure about was that everything would be very different at school, now that the young ones no longer had a teacher of their own.

'I can't see any good coming of it,' Frank said gloomily. He gazed at the high roof of the school that rose black against the sky behind them.

Andreas nodded. He looked at the silhouettes of the three farms on the St Helena Polder, and he thought of the waffles and hot chocolate that his mother would have ready for them.

Frank thought that Andreas wasn't listening. 'Come on then, what do *you* think?' he asked.

'I'll tell you,' said Andreas. He could easily look at his farm and think about school at the same time. 'When the holidays are over and we're all in the same classroom, well, then . . . ' He stopped. 'Perhaps it'll be better than we think,' he went on hesitantly.

Frank wasn't convinced. 'You must be joking!' he said scornfully. Frank was always down-to-earth. 'You're mad if you think *that*. What'll happen about the radio? And do you think those brats will understand our films? Or how a tape recorder works? Or our geography models? Or that book about the Sioux Indians? And I won't even mention the tools.' He paused to catch his breath. Frank didn't usually make long speeches.

'Yes, that's what I think too,' said Andreas. He was impressed. 'Well, then, we'll have to do something about it.'

They had reached the drive up to Andreas' house and they could smell baking waffles. They began to walk faster.

'We mustn't allow any trouble from the little ones,' Frank panted. 'And Miss Jonathan must come back.'

'But how – ' began Andreas.

'We'll have to think about that,' said Frank.

Suddenly, a large dog leapt at him from behind. The door of the house flew open and light streamed across the yard.

A cheerful voice called, 'Come on, slowcoaches! Where's the bellringer?'

Their fathers were scraping their shoes on the doorstep. Shouting joyfully, the two boys jumped on their backs. They all disappeared into the kitchen, fighting and laughing. The door closed. And outside at least seven million stars shone down, and the moon.

2. The teacher has problems

'You'd think they could be home on time just once,' Andreas' mother said on a Thursday in January as she gazed angrily into the frying pan. Andreas and Francine and Sara were already half an hour late, and feeding children was not the only thing to be done on the farm that day.

The school at Schellebelle was quite a long way from the three farms on the St Helena Polder. Every morning eight little figures on bicycles could be seen moving, slowly or fast, on the dike that led to the school. Their speed would depend on the strength of the wind which always blew over the Zeeland dikes. After that, the flapping black cape of Isaac the postman could also be glimpsed between the trees. And then the little green car of the district nurse. And, every now and again, the vet's brown jeep. Then the dike would lie quiet and empty once more until, at twelve o'clock, the same moving figures appeared against the grey sky. Two or three would turn away from the others when they reached the entrance to each farm and, an hour later, would join them again. In the afternoon, after four o'clock, they would ride past for the last time.

Anyone would think that it might be rather dull to ride along the same curved dike from home to school and from school to home four times a day. And that the children would ride as fast as they could to get the journey over with. At any rate, that's what their fathers and mothers thought. But they were wrong, of course.

The house where Andreas lived lay behind a red stone wall which divided the farm from the road. Tossing brambles grew behind the wall. The house itself was long and low with a red roof and a red front door. Behind it green trees rose, at least seventy-five tall poplars. Further on stood the enormous barn, tarred black like all Zeeland barns, with white edges round the doors and a high roof. The barn could be seen from a long way off.

'I can't imagine why it always takes you so long to get home,' Mrs Almekinders said to the potatoes in her pan. Behind her, Andreas, Francine and Sara had alighted round the table like a flock of hungry starlings. 'And it's winter, too,' she went on. 'There's no need to stop and rest because it's too hot. And you can talk to each other while you're riding. *You* were later than the others, Francine. What took you so long?'

'We had something to do on the way,' Francine

answered. She gazed hungrily at the plate her mother put in front of her.

It was pleasant in the warm kitchen, with the red geraniums on the window sill and the striped mats on the floor. The stove hummed busily near by.

'And what was that?' her mother asked. 'Don't tell me you rode round the whole polder again.'

'Frank and I were talking about bulls and oxen,' said Francine with her mouth full. 'Frank said that a bull was the husband of a cow. And I said that an ox was too. And then Frank said that was true but an ox wasn't allowed to marry a cow. And then I said – '

'The calf next door is dead,' Sara said to no one in particular. 'Why?'

Suddenly everyone took a great interest in their food and no one answered.

'I'll ask Frank, then,' said Sara crossly. 'He knows all about cows.'

'Frank won't know,' Andreas said. 'Not with all those horses at his place.' He started to eat his pudding.

'What *is* an ox, anyway?' Sara asked.

Francine sighed loudly. 'I've just told you,' she said. 'I said that an ox is the – '

'Eat up now!' her mother ordered. 'Before you know where you are it'll be time to go back to school. Here's your pudding, Sara.'

'Girls never know what they're talking about,' said Andreas.

His mother looked at him. 'How did you get that dreadful bruise, Andreas?'

Andreas went red. He grinned nervously.

'We had a race on the way home,' Francine explained. 'To see who could ride backwards the fastest.'

Andreas looked sideways at his sister. He hoped that she wouldn't tell their mother that he'd cried. Because of the pain.

'And who won?' said Mother.

'Andreas!' Sara shouted with pride. 'But he hit his head against a lamp post.'

'So *that's* why it took you so long to get home,' Mother said.

She lifted little Hendrik out of his cradle. He looked round happily, glad that lunch was on the way. He waved his hands in front of his face and then carefully examined his outspread fingers.

'He's counting!' Sara shouted. 'He's working out five plus five. I can tell him the answer!'

'Off to school with you now,' Mother laughed. 'And don't ride backwards!'

They all laughed at this, and it was clear from Andreas' thoughtful expression that his mother had given him an idea. Then they were gone. A little later seven bicycles appeared on the dike once more and, after a while, there were eight bicycles on their way to school again.

It had been very strange at school since the holidays. Miss Jonathan had gone and all the children of the school were together in one classroom now. After all, it stands to reason that the teacher couldn't let nine children stay in a room by themselves. They wouldn't behave. And so the first few days had been very strange for them all. Even the teacher found it hard to get used to.

That afternoon, he said at least nine times, 'Now, if you need me, just call me. D'you hear? And I'll help you.' He pulled funny faces for the young ones, and talked to them a lot. But he shouldn't have said anything about calling him if they needed him. For, no sooner had the little ones started writing, than Ghislain Bruynooge called: 'Sir! Sir!'

The teacher came up to him.

'Why doesn't the capital I have a dot?' Ghislain asked. He gazed fixedly at the teacher. It was obvious that the teacher didn't know the answer. Which was odd, for he taught the top classes after all.

Frank Camillemans laughed out loud.

'There's nothing to laugh at,' the teacher said firmly in his direction. Then he turned to Ghislain. 'Well, Ghislain. Look here. Well. You write it like this. And it's just a capital letter, see? That's why.'

Ghislain said nothing, but it was obvious that he wasn't satisfied. Later on, he wanted to know if fish drank water. Luckily the teacher knew the answer to that one.

Sara Almekinders had drawn a picture. The teacher looked over her shoulder curiously and saw that it was a picture of a duck.

'What's that round the duck?' he asked.

Sara laughed heartily. 'That? That's straw of course,' she said. 'But don't tell the duck. She thinks it's water.'

After that, Sara asked to be excused. She had

already put up her hand and asked at least seven times. The teacher told her she could go but Sara stayed wriggling in her seat. At last, Francine stood up and asked if she could go with her. Didn't the teacher know that Miss Jonathan always went with Sara, to help her?

'It's because he isn't married,' said Frank as they cycled home. He was right about that but, as Andreas pointed out, Frank wasn't married either and yet he had known. The boys were both feeling irritable without knowing why.

Andreas had had time to spare that afternoon because the teacher was kept so busy with the little ones. He had had enough time to write a letter to Wolfert Polderman. Before the holidays, Wolfert had sat next to him in class, but neither he nor his four brothers had come back to the school. Wolfert was the eldest. Then came Jan, Daniel, Cor and Adri. They all had red hair. The Polderman boys now went to the school in Klaaskinderkerke and each morning they caught the bus at the crossroads. But, even though they saw each other every day, Andreas still wrote his letter:

Dear Wolfert,

We still remember that you won the long jump. And when school was let out you always wanted to be the first at the door. And when you put up your hand you always twisted your wrist round. When the wind blows through the trees, I tell Frank that it is Wolfert's ghost. It is a pity that you have gone away. And your brothers too. Now we've got all the little children. Ghislain and Sara and the others. They want to be excused all the time. When we did not understand geography you always put up your hand. The place where you sat is empty. Sometimes I sit there and then my place is empty. So nothing much has happened. We are sorry that you have gone.

Best wishes from us all,

A.A.

Andreas liked the letter so much that he read it out to the others on the way home. They walked, pushing their bicycles. When Andreas had finished reading the letter, everyone agreed that they should put it in an envelope and post it.

At the bottom of the dike lay Wantje's little shop, with its glass jars. Luckily she had seven envelopes left and they could choose which of them to buy.

'Are you going to write a letter?' she asked unnecessarily.

'Well, how shall I put it? There's a good chance that we might,' said Frank carelessly. His father talked like that all the time.

Wantje sniffed. Her real name was Johanna but no one ever called her that. 'Now, don't be cheeky,' she said. 'I get enough of that from my husband. He's as cheeky as a chicken.' Her husband had never been known to move from the little room behind the shop.

'*Our* chickens are never cheeky,' Sara whispered

angrily. She always fed the chickens at home and knew what she was talking about.

They bought an envelope and stamp with Frank's money, for none of the others had any. At least, not until Saturday. And then not for long. Frank wrote the Poldermans' address on the envelope with his ballpoint. Then they posted the letter. After that, they had a contest to see who could get home with one foot on the pedal of his bicycle and the other behind the saddle. Antoine won. And that evening they were late for their meal again.

3. A letter for Andreas . . .

'There's a letter for you!' Isaac the postman shouted as he trudged into the yard with his heavy bag at his side.

Andreas, who was scraping snow from his boots at the back door, put out his hand. 'Give it to me!'

'Hold on a minute. It's not from your girl friend, you know!' Isaac answered. He liked to tease and, as Andreas watched, his grinning face disappeared inside the house.

Angrily, Andreas chased away the turkeys which had come to stare at him curiously with their round, foolish eyes. And, just as angrily, he pulled up a chair in the kitchen where everyone was drinking coffee. He had got up that morning in a bad mood and Isaac's teasing had not improved it.

'Aren't you going to say hullo?' his father asked.

Andreas did so, with a long face. Anyone would think that Isaac had never visited them before. Gilles, the farm hand, was there too. He and Isaac had served in the army together and when the two of them started on their stories about the old days,

all Andreas wanted to do was hide. But they were talking about the weather now.

Andreas drank his coffee and took a sandwich from a plate on the table. He gazed out of the window as he chewed. The polders and meadows stretched white and glittering beyond the poplars. Far in the distance, a silver ship glided past like a vision in a fairy tale. It looked as though it was floating through an endless frozen field, but Andreas knew that it was on the Schelde. Everything was white as far as the eye could see, so white that he felt that he might be blinded if he looked at it for too long. The ground was as hard as stone and the trees stood black against the brilliant snow. If Andreas half-closed his eyes he could see the roof of the Polderman house. It could just be seen above a distant dike. He couldn't see the lane that ran in front of the house. He could see it from the school during the day but now the lane was white, too, just like all the lanes and paths.

Andreas turned to face the others again. Isaac was sitting with his stockinged feet on the rung of his chair, warming his hands on his mug of coffee. It seemed that they had at last stopped talking about the weather. About how much more snow had fallen than ever before. And how it had never stayed so cold for so long before. And how fierce the snowstorms had been. And how the snow had covered some of the smaller houses up to the gutters, so high that even great-grandfathers – Andreas and Francine had one of these, he lived in Klaaskinderkerke with the aunts – could not remember deeper falls.

'There's a letter for you,' Isaac told him, as if he had never mentioned it before. 'From your friend Wolfert Polderman.' He pretended not to see Andreas' outstretched hand, and said to Father and Mother: 'So you see Brakman and Slingeling have both refused to repair the lane. It's in a dreadful state. I ruined my moped on that lane, in the tractor ruts! Anyway, because the lane's so muddy and treacherous, Polderman won't let his boys go along it to school. And it's the only way they *can* get to the school.'

'If you ask me, the Polderman boys could use Brakman's path,' said Gilles slowly. He had followed the story open-mouthed. 'The path is a nice short cut for them. It runs across Brakman's fields to the road. You can get to the school that way.' He fell silent and stuck a plug of tobacco behind his teeth.

Andreas, who had sighed loudly when his letter eluded him for a second time, pricked up his ears. This business was his concern too. Frank had arrived in the yard and was making faces at him through the window, but Andreas ignored him. And he pretended not to notice his father's mocking glance. Mr Almekinders couldn't understand why his son should suddenly be so interested in village gossip.

Francine, who could never keep her mouth closed for longer than seven minutes at a time, suddenly shouted straight through the conversation, 'Hey, Andreas! Don't sit there like an old woman. Frank's outside!'

'Now, now,' said their mother crossly. She said to Isaac: 'But surely the Water Board is responsible for keeping the lane in good order?'

Andreas had reddened. Now he would have to go. Everyone was looking at him. Slowly he pushed back his chair. 'My letter, Isaac . . . You said . . . ' He had to say that, at least, even though he would hear nothing more about the quarrel.

Isaac put the letter deliberately back in his bag and then said to Mother: 'Yes, the Water Board is responsible but they will only repair the lane when Brakman and Slingeling have paid their rates on the ditch that divides their land. But neither of them will, you see. And so the lane's got even worse after the autumn rain. You can't blame Polderman for not letting his sons go that way. And they can't even use the short cut along Brakman's path because he always chases them off it. Private property, he says. Not even a chicken can use the path, he says. He said he'll stop them once and for all, and so he has. Last night he blocked the path with a great pile of barbed wire.' Isaac took another gulp of coffee. 'Everyone's talking about it. It's bigger than anything we saw in the war. And so the Polderman boys can't use the lane or the path to get to school. And that's why they have to go in the other direction to the school at Klaaskinderkerke. Mark my words, there's worse to come yet. Last night my wife dreamed about black crows.'

Gilles' face clouded over at this. He gazed uneasily into his mug and mumbled, 'Well I never! A dream of crows. That can only mean bad luck.' He put down his mug and stood up. In his haste to leave, he forgot all about his sandwich.

'And to think that they're grown men . . . ' said Mother softly. Her gentle face looked troubled. 'Barbed wire . . . '

Isaac shrugged his shoulders and said, 'Yes, but when it's dog eat dog . . . Talking about dreams, I once dreamed that – '

Andreas tugged angrily at his sleeve. 'Can I have my letter now?' he asked irritably.

Isaac raised his eyebrows so high that Francine began to giggle nervously. Andreas reddened again, from rage this time. His mother said quickly, 'Come on, Isaac. Don't tease the boy any more. There'll be no more coffee if you do!'

The postman looked slowly in his bag. He shuffled through a pile of blue and white envelopes and, at last, gave a white envelope to Andreas. He grabbed it so quickly that Isaac shouted: 'Do you mind! I'll have my fingers back now, lad!' As Andreas left the room, he called after him: 'They don't live more than ten minutes away from each other and yet they write letters! And I've got to struggle through the snow on my old legs to deliver them!'

Andreas didn't hear him. Francine followed him, a piece of pancake in her hand.

'Andreas!' she shouted. 'Can I read what it says?'

Andreas didn't answer. He was busy putting on his clogs. His wet boots were lying in the yard where he had kicked them earlier. It certainly didn't look as if he would take her with him.

'Where are you going, Andreas? Can I come too?' she asked hopefully.

'No,' said her brother. 'Girls always give the game away.'

Francine's mouth fell open in astonishment. 'Well, that's a cheek, I must say!' she shouted. Then she softened her tone. 'Can't I come with you to Frank's?'

'No,' said Andreas firmly. 'Girls can't keep secrets.'

'So that's what you think, is it?' said Francine loftily. 'If you only had enough sense you'd know that we're better at keeping secrets than you think. Better than Frank even.' She was really angry now.

'So what? I've got to talk about this with Frank

first,' said Andreas. 'So go and do your knitting or something.'

Francine could see that neither flattery nor insults would change his mind. But she couldn't understand it. He wasn't usually so annoying. She put her finger in her mouth as she watched Andreas. She always did this when she had something serious to think about. One of her teeth was loose.

The door creaked behind her and Isaac stamped outside. 'Don't stand there in the cold, girl,' he said in a fatherly way. He rubbed his hands, tied his scarf firmly round his neck and waded through the snow to the road. His breath danced in front of him like a plume of smoke. Then Francine saw him pass along the high dike. He looked like a giant kangaroo with his letter bag on his stomach.

'Well, I'm off!' Andreas shouted from the yard.

'Be home in time,' his mother called back.

Francine looked angrily at her brother. 'Be careful, little boy!' she jeered.

Brothers! It was always like this. You played together for years, and made plans together. And then, all at once, they wanted to be by themselves. They said that girls didn't dare to climb on the beams in the barn. Or feel in the straw for young kittens, to save them from rats. Or jump over the ditch, or test the ice on the pond. Francine wrinkled her nose in contempt. What did it matter if she wouldn't swing a dead rat round and round by the tail, like Antoine next door. Or sign her name in blood on secret documents to be buried and found again on purpose. Or play Indians and scalp someone. But then *she* didn't sit about looking like a sick fish when strangers were in the house. Just wait. She'd go and see Jeanne-Marie. And she'd never speak to Andreas again. Not for a whole week. And not on the way to school either. And she'd have nothing to do with him at school when they dug caves in the snow in which the girls, who were the smugglers, would be imprisoned by the boys, who were always the customs men. She'd ask Jeanne-Marie and Marie-Madeleine not to speak to the boys either. Not for a whole week. Perhaps for longer. And certainly not at school.

She wished suddenly that Miss Jonathan would come back to the school. It wasn't any fun without her. She felt very sure of that as she stood in the cold farmyard. But she realized at the same time that there was little chance that Miss Jonathan would come back. She had understood that from what she had heard in the kitchen. Francine sighed.

She sighed again when she heard light footsteps drumming on the frozen drive. A girl with black plaits trotted into the yard. Another girl ran a few yards behind her. A voice shouted excitedly, 'Francine! Francine!'

It was Jeanne-Marie. And she was waving something white above her head.

4. . . . and one for Jeanne-Marie

As well as Reigershof farm, where Frank Camillemans and the twenty horses lived, and Plankenpoortje farm, where Andreas lived, there was one other farm in the St Helena Polder. It was called Stellahoeve and Francine's friends lived there. Jeanne-Marie was ten years old and Marie-Madeleine was nine. All the girls in the Rosseel family had been given those names ever since the day that the first Jeanne-Marie had fled from France to live there. That had happened a very long time ago, of course.

Jeanne-Marie and Marie-Madeleine both had dark hair and brown eyes, and golden brown skins. They were friendly but shy, especially Marie-Madeleine. Francine didn't know which of them she liked the most. The three girls often spent the night at each other's houses. And they wrote little verses in each other's autograph albums. Between them, they had thirteen dolls. Jeanne-Marie and Marie-Madeleine also had a brother, Antoine, who sat next to Frank at school. Antoine was small, with pitch black eyes and black curly hair, and he could run even faster than Frank. He wasn't shy, like his sisters, but he wasn't very friendly either.

That morning a letter had come for Jeanne-Marie, the first she had ever received addressed to her alone. She had turned it over, looking around uncertainly. They were slaughtering on the farm that day and no one had had time to notice her. Mother was so busy that even Isaac the postman had left without a cup of coffee. The kitchen and scullery were crowded with tubs full of chunks of red meat, ready to be put in the deep freeze. The butcher from Klaaskinderkerke, with his bloodstained apron, was busy making sausages and Mother was stirring brawn in a big pan, her dark hair falling over her eyes. Antoine was watching it all with interest, but not his sisters. They hated everything to do with slaughtering, and Jeanne-Marie was frightened of the butcher who always asked her if she had found a boy friend yet. Every year they were furious with their father for not sparing the pigs, the pigs that had been such dear little piglets in the spring, as small as toy animals and as soft as silk.

Jeanne-Marie had fidgeted with her letter for so long that at last Marie-Madeleine had said, 'Come on, let's show it to Francine.'

Now the three girls stood talking excitedly in the wide white yard of Plankenpoortje farm, by the frozen pond under the willows. Jeanne-Marie started to open her letter but Francine stopped her, peered round suspiciously with her fingers on her lips, and pulled the sisters after her into the wash house.

'Read it out loud,' she whispered. And Jeanne-Marie read:

INTERNATIONAL CHAIN LETTER

Within three days, send a copy of this letter to six of your friends. Then send a postcard to the first individual on the following list. When you have copied out this letter, cross out the first name on the list and put down your own name as number six. In about six weeks time you will receive five hundred postcards. You will be surprised to see where they all come from. If you do not wish to join in, send the letter back as quickly as possible or else you will break the chain. It is very important that the chain should not be broken for some of us are ill. And it means a lot to us.

At the bottom of the letter were five names that Jeanne-Marie had never seen before. But the last name was Jessica from the Manse, who must have been the one who sent the letter to Jeanne-Marie. They weren't quite sure what they had to do. To begin with, they didn't know what 'international' meant or, for that matter, 'individual'. Those words hadn't yet come up in dictation at school. So they decided to keep the letter a secret for the time being.

'Perhaps it's got something to do with Wolfert

Polderman's letter,' Francine said excitedly. 'It's strange that we should have two letters in one day.'

The others agreed. Jeanne-Marie put the letter carefully into her pocket.

'What a wonderful thing to happen, even if you *aren't* ill,' said Marie-Madeleine dreamily. 'Just think, five hundred postcards! But Jessica isn't ill. I saw her in the village yesterday. So perhaps the other five are the ill ones.'

'Well, we must do something about it,' said Jeanne-Marie. 'I wonder if Wantje has any postcards in her shop . . . '

At that moment there was a noise outside, and a teasing voice called through the broken wash house window, 'Can we read it too?'

'An individual just means a person!' another voice shouted.

Then there was the sound of stifled laughter.

'That's Frank!' Francine said angrily. 'But I bet he doesn't know what "international" means.'

She looked out of the window and was just in time to see two figures running across the yard. 'Sneaks!' she shouted after them through the broken pane.

Behind the three farmhouses the land stretched as far as the eye could see. It was so white and wide that it was impossible to tell where the land belonging to Mr Almekinders ended and that of Mr Camillemans began. Only the black barn roofs could be seen against the snow. And the abandoned car which lay in one of the fields. The workers often ate their lunch there in the summer, and sheltered in it when it rained. The children often played in it too, but, at this time of year, few people came there. The fields lay white and dead around it, and the car itself wore a thick cap of snow. From a long way away it looked like an angry old man sitting in the field.

Andreas sat inside the car and read out his letter, just as Jeanne-Marie had read hers.

'A lot of fuss about nothing,' said Frank irritably when the letter was finished. He wasn't thinking about the letter but about the quarrel with the girls.

'It's all right for them, riding in the bus every

day,' Andreas said. He thought Frank was talking about the Poldermans and about the situation at school.

'Let's see it,' Frank said curtly.

Andreas passed the letter to him. It had been typed on the back of a page torn from a calendar advertising animal feeds, and the picture of cockerels on the other side showed through. Gloomily, Frank read:

DearAllhowareyouwearefineherewewishwewerestillthere tootheyteaseusheremeandJanIamtypingthisontheteachers machinebutIwontalwaysbeableto.thebusskiddedoneday butwewereallrightinthefront.howarethingsatthebest schoolinSchellebellewedoalotofsumshere.todaytheteacher cametoseeourmothershedidnotsaywhybutsheisalsofedup withitbutitisgreatinthebusaslongasitdoesnotskidwewish wewerebackisJansdeskstillempty,?, sinceregreetingsfrom theundersignedyourfriendWolfert.

'I bet he didn't think up that last bit himself,' Frank said critically. 'Does a typewriter always write like that, with the words so close together?'

'Who cares?' said Andreas grumpily. He was becoming steadily more bad-tempered and the Polderman experiences with typewriters and skidding buses had done nothing to improve his mood. 'At least they don't like it there,' he said.

'That's true enough,' said Frank grimly. He put the letter in his pocket.

'Hey, stop pushing,' said Andreas.

'I'm not doing anything,' said Frank peevishly.

'You are, you're pushing,' said Andreas.

They stared through the car windows in silence. They felt hypnotized by the ghostly loneliness of the ice-hard countryside that glistened around them. Andreas looked at his friend. And Frank, who understood the reasons for Andreas' moodiness, said suddenly, 'We've got to get Miss Jonathan back. That's what *I* think, anyway.'

They began to whisper excitedly. By the time they raced back to their farms across the snow, darkness was falling. And seven million stars shone once again in the black sky.

'We've got to get Miss Jonathan back,' said Wantje, at the exact moment Frank was saying it in the abandoned car.

Wantje was very old indeed but she could remember what school had been like when she was a little girl. There had been seventy children in those days, and two lady teachers. And a schoolmaster with a long beard.

Francine and Jeanne-Marie sat on the little bench in Wantje's shop, swinging their legs. Marie-Madeleine had stayed at home to find a safe hiding place for the letter. The other two girls, meanwhile, had bought a postcard and a stamp, returned a library book for Francine's mother and bought a kilo of sugar for her. They had also bought plastic bags, a mop, a packet of coffee and a cake for Jeanne-Marie's mother.

Wantje was very old and very small. Her house was very small too, and so was the lending library which she kept in the shop. For as long as anyone could remember, Wantje had had a great many books. Long ago, people had started to borrow them. In the end so many people did this that someone told her, 'You should charge people for borrowing them, Wantje.'

'That's a good idea,' Wantje had said. 'But I'll put the money in my box.'

Wantje had a collecting box in her shop in aid of the children's hospital. When, at last, everyone in Schellebelle had read all her books, Wantje raised the reading fee by one cent and used the money to buy new books. She was seventy-eight years old now and people still came to borrow her books. And when she wasn't weighing sugar or salt and filling glass jars with bulls-eyes, she would sort through her library tickets. Which is what she was doing now.

The two girls had been watching her in silence, sucking bulls-eyes which Wantje had given them. They gazed at Wantje's old face, her wrinkled hands, and her library tickets. Their mothers said that Wantje had been doing the same things for forty years. Francine added her own age to Jeanne-Marie's, and then to Andreas', and little Hendrik's. But the total was nowhere near forty.

Wantje looked up. Even though Francine hadn't spoken her thoughts aloud, Wantje said, 'People say to me, how can you bear to do the same things every day of your life? But if I didn't do them I'd be a forgotten old lady. But I'm not, am I? And it's a nice little job and I've plenty of customers. There's been as many as four cars parked outside before now. It's as friendly here as it is at the barber's. And I'm open every day until eight o'clock.' She gestured towards the frosty dike outside the window. 'People have been reading lots of my books in this cold weather,' she went on proudly. ' "Oh, you *have* got nice books, Wantje," they say. Which is true, for I only buy the best. "What a pity you live so far away," they say. Only the other day, Miss Jonathan came in . . . '

She stopped, and peered closely at the girls for the first time. She saw that Francine, who was usually so lively, was staring sadly at the gleaming glass jars with her finger in her mouth. Jeanne-Marie, too, was silent.

'What are you staring at?' Wantje asked.

'I was just thinking,' answered Jeanne-Marie. She was always very polite.

Francine thought angrily: Wantje's been talking for a quarter of an hour without noticing us, and now she asks us what we're staring at. Aloud she said, 'There's nothing else to do.'

Francine was in a bad mood which seemed to be

getting worse. She wasn't sure if this was because the boys had listened to Jeanne-Marie's letter, or because Andreas had refused to show her *his* letter. 'Take no notice,' her mother always said. 'Sooner or later they'll come back by themselves.' But it was easy for mothers to talk. *They* had had a lady teacher. And seventy children at school with them.

Suddenly Francine sat up straight, her feet firmly on the black-and-white tiled floor. She pulled her finger from her mouth and with it came the loose tooth. Francine gazed at it, frowning. She knew now why she was so depressed. It had nothing to do with the boys. It was because of Miss Jonathan. Why, oh why, had she gone away?

Wantje had put away her library tickets. She peered at the children over her steel glasses, her clear blue eyes surrounded by a sea of wrinkles. Her old voice sounded very firm and clear as she said:

'We've got to get Miss Jonathan back. A school is nothing without a lady teacher.'

Francine and Jeanne-Marie nodded. So Wantje thought so too? They looked curiously at her. Her face looked the same but, for a moment, it had seemed as though she was as young as they were. Now, for the first time, the two girls realized how much they missed Miss Jonathan.

It seemed as though Wantje could read their thoughts. She said, 'Well, you must see that she comes back. Girls need a lady teacher. How else will you learn to knit?'

It was strange that such an old lady could know exactly how different a school could be without a lady teacher. Knitting had nothing to do with it, really.

Jeanne-Marie, usually so shy, said, 'Yes, but how can we? Miss Jonathan's gone. She's in Klaaskinderkerke now.'

'I said that you must see that she comes back,' the old lady answered. 'It's what you want, isn't it?'

'Yes, of course,' said Francine. Surely Wantje knew that it wasn't as easy as that? 'There aren't enough children in the school now,' she went on. 'Everyone knows that. Four families have moved to the town, to the factory. And two have gone to help build the new bridge over the Schelde. And the Polderman boys have gone to another school.'

'Why have they gone?' said Wantje calmly. 'There's been a quarrel, hasn't there?'

The girls nodded vaguely.

Wantje sniffed and adjusted her glasses. 'Here's a book for your mother. She hasn't had it before. It's a good one, tell her. Everyone else has had a nice cry over it. And Miss Jonathan must come back. A school is nothing without a lady teacher.'

The door of the shop opened and a man came inside.

'If only we knew how,' said Francine hesitantly.

'If you want something badly enough, you'll get it,' said Wantje. The man looked at her uneasily. Wantje took no notice of him. She fingered her coral necklace and looked sharply at the children over her glasses.

'How?' she said. 'Well, you must work that out for yourselves.'

5. Questions

For days, no, weeks, it had seemed that the school at Schellebelle had changed forever. The children were different, too. And the teacher. The atmosphere in the classroom was different. It was more nervous. More irritable. Whenever the girls started pushing each other, the teacher would look up in annoyance from the desk where he was helping Ghislain or Sara with the letter 'f' or the figure '5'. He didn't joke about fighting fishwives as he used to. He just looked angry, which frightened the younger girls. He didn't have as much time now to look at the geography scrap books of the older children. He hadn't looked at Frank's book for over two weeks. The teacher was often bad-tempered, too, which wasn't like him at all. He had taken to wiping his forehead with a big white handkerchief, especially when he had finished explaining things to Ghislain.

On Wednesday morning, when Antoine Rosseel, despite repeated warnings, continued to giggle and whisper with the other boys, the teacher lost his temper completely. He marched up to Antoine's desk and was just in time to see Andreas trying to hide a note which he was about to pass to Antoine. Andreas was frightened. He crumpled the note behind his back but the teacher had seen it.

'Give me that rubbish,' the teacher snapped.

Andreas did not move. The teacher said nothing, but his face became so angry that the girls put their hands in front of their mouths. The entire first class stood up to see what was happening. And the third class, including Francine and Marie-Madeleine, looked anxiously back at the fourth. The second class did nothing because there wasn't one.

'I see. You won't give it to me?' the teacher asked icily.

Andreas shook his head. His face was as red as a beetroot. He could be very obstinate. But his obstinacy seemed to increase the teacher's anger. He jerked Andreas from his desk so suddenly that the note drifted to the floor. The teacher picked it up and read it. The whole class watched in silence.

Francine had turned very pale. And Marie-Madeleine didn't dare to look at the teacher. Jeanne-Marie stared straight at Andreas. He was gazing at the floorboards, redfaced and surly. You would have heard a pin drop, if anyone had dropped one, which no one did.

'Andreas,' said the teacher. His voice sounded odd, as if he was trying to suppress something.

Andreas shuffled. He stood there, big and

obstinate and angry, and Jeanne-Marie could not take her eyes away from him.

'Andreas,' said the teacher again.

Andreas looked up carefully through his tangled yellow fringe. And then a sigh of relief ran through the class. They could see now that the teacher was trying hard not to laugh. Andreas saw it too. All the same, his answer when it came was sulky: 'Yes, sir.'

'It's very well written,' the teacher continued sternly. 'Not a single mistake. But then that's only to be expected. You've always been good at grammar. But . . . '

And then he could control himself no longer. He burst into great roars of laughter. And the children, who didn't really know what was happening, laughed too. It was the laughter of relief. Andreas had probably written a rude word. Or *Janne loves Jan* or *The person who reads this is a fool.* It didn't really matter. They bellowed with laughter, their mouths open and their eyes closed.

Then the teacher raised his hand. 'Listen,' he said. 'I'll . . . ' Then he looked at Andreas, who shook his head almost imperceptibly. And the teacher said, 'No, I can't read private letters out to the class. I almost forgot. Here you are, Andreas. All right, children, that's enough laughter for today. It's play time.' He mopped his eyes with the white handkerchief. It was becoming quite grubby, Marie-Madeleine noticed.

Outside, all the children immediately congregated around Andreas but Frank and Antoine chased the girls and little ones away. They retreated to the gate and jeered at the boys from a safe distance. The five older boys then crept behind the garage that the teacher had built next to the school house and which was now buried in snow. Andreas produced his note and read it out loud:

Why can't houses walk?
Why can't flies walk backwards?
Why do they always bury dead people in cemeteries?
Why is it so dark at night?
Why doesn't a worm have any ears?
Does grandfather have birthdays in his grave?
Why is the sea so wet?

The boys rolled about in the snow, howling with laughter.

'How do they think them up?' shouted Frank. ' "Why doesn't a worm have any ears!" '

'It's all very well to laugh,' said Andreas bitterly. 'Those are just questions that the little ones asked this morning. But it's like that all day now. And then they're always asking to be excused. The teacher doesn't have any time for us now. We haven't touched the recorders for weeks, and we've had no volleyball or anything. I'm fed up with it.'

'The teacher's fed up with it too,' Antoine said

suddenly. 'And it's true about the recorders.' Only that morning his mother had asked him why he hadn't been practising recently. She liked recorder music, even though Antoine was always sent outside to practise.

'Do you really think so?' asked Andreas hopefully.

'Of course, especially now that Miss Jonathan won't be coming back. He's been hoping she will, like all of us.'

The others nodded, and fell silent. Then Frank said, 'Look, now that he knows that we've had enough of it, we can ask him what to do about the quarrel.'

He looked at Andreas, who nodded, and then told the others what he and Andreas had agreed in the abandoned car the day before. They would set up a Society for the Eradication of Feuds in order to settle the quarrel that had resulted in the Polderman boys leaving the school. They knew now that Miss Jonathan could only come back if the Poldermans returned first. Frank had found the name of the society in an agricultural journal. They had changed 'parasites' to 'feuds' and left out a bit at the end about insect control. Andreas had wanted to leave that in but Frank had overruled him.

The boys looked at each other. Then they stood up, brushed the snow from their clothes and went back towards the school. The girls watched them resentfully as they passed. Inside the classroom, the teacher was giving out books and turned round immediately when Frank coughed.

Frank said, 'Sir, how many children must there be in the school before Miss Jonathan comes back?'

'Thirty-one,' the teacher answered. He rubbed his brow and said, 'Go and sit down, boys.'

They did so, and the teacher sat on his table. His long legs swung back and forth. He looked like an old friend when he sat like that. He wasn't really old. Twenty-five perhaps. He had black hair and eyes. He always wore a blue sweater over his white shirt, and he smoked an old pipe. The boys felt completely at ease with him now. It used to be like this before the Christmas holidays when they made things together and recorded the language lessons on the tape recorder.

The teacher listened carefully as Andreas told him about the Society for the Eradication of Feuds. When he had finished, Antoine said, 'It would be best if we found out what really happened. What they quarrelled about. And who quarrelled with whom.'

The teacher took his pipe out of his mouth and looked with interest at the glowing tobacco. His tobacco smelt good. There was a pattern of red and green diamonds on the packet, and an English word.

'Yes,' he said. 'But it won't be as simple as that. People quarrel about the strangest things.'

The boys nodded. They had always known that

grown-ups quarrel too. After all, they weren't deaf, even though grown-ups seemed to think that they were at times. They knew, too, that grown-up quarrels could last for a very long time and that it was dangerous to interfere. They knew all about that.

Andreas said, 'We've got to try. It can't go on like this much longer.'

The teacher said nothing. He blew out a cloud of smoke.

'The difficult thing,' said Frank slowly, 'is that one quarrel is joined to another.'

The teacher nodded. There was a satisfied expression on his face.

'We know that,' said Andreas. 'And that's why we've formed the Society. So we can collect signatures and things.' He wasn't really sure what the Society was going to do but he had read somewhere about a group of people who had collected thousands of signatures for some reason. 'That'll put an end to it,' he added cryptically.

The others nodded.

'Wouldn't it be easier to kidnap the Poldermans?' Antoine asked hopefully.

'No,' said Frank.

'Then we could force the other school to let them come back,' Antoine went on.

'It's too difficult,' said Frank, who had already discarded this idea. He liked to consider matters from every angle, unlike Antoine who thought that all problems could be solved by fighting. Antoine was often in trouble because of this and spent a great deal of time locked in the loft at home as a punishment. Whenever this happened he had to shell beans. Antoine had become so skilful at shelling beans that he usually had time over to read while the rain drummed on the roof and murmured in the gutters. He had a fine collection of cowboy books which he kept in the loft.

The teacher continued to smoke in silence. He peered through the smoke at the boys who didn't seem to realize he was there any more. They were now so excited that they would have liked to have started on the project at once.

'We'll meet at four o'clock,' Andreas said loudly.

The teacher raised his hand. 'What I want to know,' he said calmly, 'is why you wrote down all those questions, Andreas.'

Andreas fell silent with embarrassment. 'Well,' he said uneasily, 'I had some time left over. All those questions they ask. And no answers either. I was going to ask my mother. Sara often asks things like that at home.'

'A good idea,' said the teacher. 'And then come and tell *me* what the answers are.' He puffed at his pipe. 'Little children need a lady teacher,' he said. 'You're not the only ones who are going short. "Why doesn't a worm have ears?" Now I ask you!'

Suddenly a head appeared at one of the windows. They all saw it quickly disappear.

'Francine!' Andreas shouted angrily. 'The girls are always snooping!' He had forgotten that, only yesterday, he and Frank had stood listening at the wash house window. From outside came the sound of a dull thud, followed by a tearful wail.

The teacher stood up. 'Here's a piece of paper,' he said. 'It's a bit bigger than your note, Andreas. Write down the reasons for your plan. And then the plan itself. You must always work things out carefully in advance. Like this.' He went to the blackboard and wrote on it with thick yellow chalk: *The reasons why there is no longer a schoolmistress at Schellebelle.*

'Well, Frank?' he asked.

'Because the Polderman boys have gone to another school,' droned Frank. You could see that he knew what the teacher was getting at.

The teacher wrote: *The reasons why the Poldermans have gone.*

'Antoine!' he said.

Antoine roared, 'There's been a quarrel.'

Again the teacher wrote: *The reasons why there has been a quarrel.*

'Andreas!'

After a slight hesitation, Andreas said, 'Under investigation.'

'Splendid!' said the teacher, and cleaned the

board with his sleeve. He turned and saw the disappointment on the faces of the boys.

'But how does it go on from there?' two of them asked at once.

'Sorting out the quarrel, d'you mean?' asked the teacher. 'Well, that's something you'll have to do for yourselves.'

He sent the boys to their desks and then rang the bell as if his life depended on it. A little later, all the children were sitting, rosy and panting, in their places. There were twenty-six children altogether, big ones and small ones, tall and short ones, fat and thin ones. Children with freckles and without freckles, children with curly hair and children with straight hair, wet from snowballing. And two with glasses.

Andreas put up his hand.

'Yes, Andreas?' said the teacher.

'I only want to ask one thing,' said Andreas. 'Has it ever happened before?'

Francine turned round and stared wide-eyed at her brother. What on earth was he talking about? But the teacher seemed to understand. He answered, just as mysteriously, 'Yes, once, but it's some time ago now. We lost five then. So we don't want it to happen again if we can help it. Understand?'

'Yes, sir,' said Andreas. His face shone. His eyes sparkled. He hasn't looked so happy for weeks, thought Francine jealously. Even Frank, usually so self-controlled, looked elated. Antoine was rubbing his hands together, obviously thinking of a good fight.

Sara put up her hand.

'Yes, Sara?' said the teacher patiently.

'Sir, when all the people in the village are dead, what will they do with the houses, sir?'

Andreas sighed loudly. But the teacher said cheerfully, 'Well, Sara . . . well . . . er . . . then the children who are small now will go and live in them. And those who've only just been born. Like Hendrik. Understand?'

'Yes, sir,' said Sara, satisfied. She bent over her exercise book and began to write the 'f' and the 'g'. She didn't notice the gentle smiles of the older children.

Then Andreas put up his hand. 'Sir, why – ' he began. And he couldn't understand why everyone round him burst out laughing.

6. Antoine and Mr Brakman

It had stopped snowing when they came out of school. A gentle rain was falling now and this seemed strange after so many weeks of ice and snow. It was still cold, though, and the breath of the running boys and girls danced in the air like smoke.

'Come on!' panted Andreas. 'We've only got a couple of hours. Everyone will be busy milking so it's a good time to find things out.'

They did not follow their usual route along the dike but turned instead down the lane that ran past the Polderman house. A high tree-covered dike rose to their left and on the right, behind a wide ditch, lay two farms and a handful of scattered houses with pointed roofs.

As they passed Mr Brakman's black wooden barn, his son Leendert came into the yard. He was pushing a wheelbarrow full of straw and stopped to grin mockingly at the children. He had left school the year before.

'You walk on,' Antoine called to the others. 'I'll catch you up.'

He walked towards Leendert. 'When are you

going to get rid of that stupid barbed wire on your path?' he said.

Leendert seemed taken aback. Then a sly smile spread across his face. 'It'll stay there as long as we want it to,' he answered.

'Then you're a blockhead! You haven't heard the last of this, you know.' Antoine had overheard the village policeman say this to one of the local drunks. It sounded quite impressive, he thought. He ran on after the other children.

'Mind your own business!' Leendert shouted after him.

Antoine caught up with the others and slowed to a walk. He felt on top of the world. Nothing could stop them now.

Andreas was telling the girls about the Society, and what the teacher had said. 'We'll sort it all out this evening,' he finished. 'That's what the Society's for. We'll have to be very cunning, of course, but we'll get to the bottom of it.' He paused to catch his breath. 'By fair means or foul,' he added dramatically.

Francine said sharply that foul means would only bring more trouble and that she and the other girls would prefer the fair means, if he didn't mind. Marie-Madeleine and Jeanne-Marie nodded, and Francine said that they couldn't just burst into Mr Polderman's house and ask him why he'd quarrelled with Mr Brakman. He'd throw them out as soon as look at them. And he probably wouldn't be at home anyway.

Frank said, 'But who said that he *has* quarrelled with Brakman?'

The children stopped, taken aback. Frank was usually so quiet but every now and then he would come out with a question that floored the others completely.

'Yes, who did?' said Andreas, turning to look at Frank. He lost his balance and fell flat on the snow-covered lane, dragging Antoine with him. They scrambled to their feet.

'You've got something there,' Antoine said.

'We can't be sure whether they've quarrelled or not,' Jeanne-Marie said sensibly.

'It seems very unlikely to me.' This came from Marie-Madeleine.

Andreas brushed snow from his trousers and said excitedly, 'Now you mention it, it does seem unlikely.'

'Well, even if Mr Polderman didn't quarrel with Brakman, he's still taken his boys away from our school,' said Francine. She blew into her hands. 'How much longer are we going to stand here, anyway?'

Flakes of wet snow drifted down from the branches overhead. Francine looked up, and Antoine followed her gaze. 'It's starting to thaw,' he said to no one in particular.

The others didn't answer. They stood frowning and shivering, their heads sunk deep in their collars. What on earth were they going to do now? All they could be sure of was that someone had quarrelled with someone else. But then there were always quarrels going on in the village. They were usually about boundary hedges. Or ditches. Or rows of trees. Or about who was going to inherit a piece of land when grandpa died.

'We've got to make a start,' Andreas announced suddenly. 'Come on, we've got to do something.' He beckoned Frank and Antoine to follow him.

'What about us, then?' Francine shouted shrilly.

'Oh yes, the girls,' said Andreas, as if he was seeing them for the first time.

'Why can't we join in too?' Francine went on.

'Yes, why can't we?' said Jeanne-Marie. She was not as shy as Marie-Madeleine but it took all her courage to talk to Andreas like that.

Frank looked at Marie-Madeleine's cold face. 'Let them come too, if they want,' he said grudgingly.

'Oh, all right,' said Andreas. 'But I'm the leader. It was my idea.'

Everyone agreed to this. They were all relieved to be friends again.

Andreas said in a business-like tone, 'The girls had better go back to the end of the lane. We'll start our investigations here. We'll meet in the old car before supper and compare notes.'

'Why can't we all go together?' asked Francine.

'It'll look suspicious if we do. It'll be better if we work separately.' It seemed to Andreas that the girls didn't share his enthusiasm.

'How far are we going?' said Antoine briskly.

'Until we've found the quarrel,' Andreas said firmly. He turned to the girls and said, 'You can go where you like. Not to the Poldermans, of course.'

'And don't go near Old Pier,' said Antoine. 'You know he's a bit wrong in the head.'

The boys winked at each other and then ran off so unexpectedly that tears sprang into Francine's eyes. The girls stood in the lane, cold and bewildered.

'It's not *fair*!' Francine said. Oh, why did the boys never let them join in?

Marie-Madeleine saw her tears. 'Don't cry,' she said. 'I know what we'll do.'

'What?' asked Francine sulkily.

Marie-Madeleine pulled the two girls closer to her, and lowered her voice. She said mysteriously, 'You remember the chain letter?'

Francine and Jeanne-Marie nodded.

'Well,' Marie-Madeleine continued softly. 'Every day we'll write out a few postcards and send them to Mr Polderman.'

'I don't understand,' said Francine hesitantly. A tear still clung to her cheek.

Jeanne-Marie dug her cheerfully in the ribs. 'If someone sends you five hundred postcards,' she said, 'then it must mean that they aren't angry with you any more.'

'So we find out who Polderman quarrelled with and put down whoever it was as the sender?'

'Exactly!' shouted Jeanne-Marie. She giggled with anticipation. 'Can't you just see his face? You can't stay cross with someone who sends you five hundred postcards!'

Laughing excitedly, the girls started to run down the lane. They had forgotten all about the boys. And, in their excitement, they didn't notice two small figures coming out of the school.

Ghislain and Sara had stayed behind to help the teacher to clear up. They watched the girls rush past and waited, undecided, on the broad dike road. A moped came towards them, driven by a man. When he reached the children he came to a stop.

'D'you know where I can find the St Marguerite Polder?' he asked irritably. 'It's somewhere round here, I think.'

'No, I don't,' said Sara. She held Ghislain's hand and stared at the man curiously.

'Then you're a stupid girl!' the man said angrily. He lurched away down the road.

Ghislain gave Sara a push. 'He said you were stupid. But he didn't even know the answer himself!'

Laughing loudly, they began to walk home. Above them hung the dripping branches of the trees and every now and then clumps of wet snow fell at their feet. A hungry hare suddenly bounded across the road in search of food. The polder stretched wide and white and silent ahead of them.

Andreas came to a sudden halt in the lane. In front of him, a thin string of smoke drifted from a chimney. Under the chimney lived the Poldermans. He knew their house well. But it looked different now that he was about to try to solve the mystery of the quarrel.

The three boys had realized now that their task would be much harder than they had anticipated.

'If only we could beat up the person who started it all,' Antoine said wistfully.

'Violence wouldn't solve anything,' said Frank.

'I agree,' said Andreas. 'Now, let's reconnoitre the scene of the crime.'

Not far from the Poldermans' house a narrow path ran across the fields. It led from the lane to the road near the school. That is to say, it *used* to lead to the road. Now a strange snow-covered hill blocked the path completely. This was the pile of barbed wire that Isaac the postman had spoken about. It was now impossible to use the path as a short cut to the main road.

The boys gazed at the path in silence.

'So that's what Brakman's done,' murmured Frank. 'If only he hadn't.'

'Yes, if only,' said Antoine. His fists were itching.

'Let's see how heavy the wire is,' said Andreas. 'You never know.' He brushed away a little of the snow. 'It's beginning to rust. That's promising.'

Antoine took a flying leap on to the top of the little hill. The others followed, and rocked precariously on the summit.

'Come on, men!' roared Antoine. 'For the motherland! Man the barricades! Up Robespierre, up Danton! Follow me! Liberty, equality . . . '

The word 'fraternity' froze on his lips as a furious voice shouted, 'First you cheek my son! And now you're trespassing on my land!'

Antoine went pale. Mr Brakman had appeared between the willows which grew along the track. 'All right, what are you doing on my property?' he thundered. 'And in broad daylight too!'

The boys didn't move. Antoine thought about running away but there seemed little point.

'We were only . . . ' began Andreas, and then stopped. What could he say? That they were inspecting the barbed wire barricade?

Brakman was closer now. 'Well,' he shouted. 'It isn't those Polderman brats after all. They've got red hair. And you're smaller. Well, you've still got me to reckon with!'

The farmer was so angry that the boys began to feel afraid. He stood with his arms akimbo and it was obvious that they wouldn't be able to get away very easily. He looked ridiculous, really, with his little fierce eyes and his large cropped head. His ears were very large. But, all the same, none of the boys felt like laughing. One of Brakman's enormous red hands grasped Antoine's leg and pulled him to the ground.

'Fraternity, hey?' Brakman sneered. 'It's easy to see that your forefathers were French. You're all the same.' He pushed Antoine ahead of him up the track. 'As you're so fond of shouting at my son, you'd better come with me. No, not you!' he shouted angrily over his shoulder at Andreas and Frank who were following.

The boys leaped back. But as soon as Brakman had turned his head, they caught up with him again. This went on for some time, with Brakman abusing the boys over his shoulder and Andreas and Frank clinging to his heels like terriers.

They reached the farm and were confronted by Leendert who shouted triumphantly, 'Get off! I'll set the dog on you!'

This was an unconvincing threat. The boys knew that the Brakmans' dog couldn't frighten a rat and, in any case, she liked them more than she did the Brakmans.

The farmer dragged Antoine through the gate and slammed it in the faces of the two boys. Chickens flapped angrily away on stick-like legs.

'Look, sir, we weren't doing anything,' Andreas said as politely as he could.

'Pull the other one,' Brakman said grimly through the railings. 'You were trespassing. I could run you in for that alone. But this ruffian here's always cheeking my son. And I haven't forgotten about him and my pear trees . . . ' He disappeared into the house, leaving the boys clutching the gate in the dusk.

'Bully!' Andreas shouted angrily.

Frank looked at him doubtfully and then cupped his hands over his mouth and bellowed, 'Kid-napper!'

The door flew open and Leendert shouted, 'Clear off! Or he'll stay here for the rest of his life!'

'Pick on someone your own size!' shouted Frank. They exhausted their stock of swearwords and fell silent.

'Let's see if we can find out where he is,' muttered Andreas. They followed the fence round the side of the house. When they reached the back, Andreas peered upwards. A white curtain was flapping from an open window. Frank whistled softly.

'What are you doing now?' Andreas whispered. He was shivering.

'Sssh!' said Frank.

A head covered with grey hair and a white cap appeared at the window. A muffled voice said, 'Go away. If he sees you . . . '

'He's seen us already,' said Frank politely. 'We didn't do anything.' He whispered to Andreas, 'It's old Krina. She knows me.' Aloud he said, 'Listen Krina, can you tell us – '

A second window creaked open and Leendert's grinning face appeared.

'Where is he?' said Andreas.

'In the cupboard,' said the old lady.

'He's in the cupboard and he'll stay there forever!' jeered Leendert. 'With bread and water!'

'What do you want?' whispered Krina. 'There'll be trouble . . . '

'We want our friend back,' said Andreas loudly. 'Now.'

Krina nearly fell from her window with alarm.

'Our fathers are coming,' Andreas shouted. 'Frank called them. And they'll let him out if you don't do it now. And I mean *now*.'

The old housekeeper began to wave her arms about so wildly that Frank felt sure she would fall into the yard.

'We're waiting,' said Andreas grimly.

Krina called, 'If you go away, if you'll only go . . . I'll see what I can do . . . if you'll only . . . '

'Out of the question,' said Andreas firmly. 'We're staying put till our fathers get here. They won't be long now.'

'There'll be a fight.' Krina was crying now.

'I expect there will,' said Andreas carelessly. 'So what?'

'Then the police will come. He said so himself.'

The window closed suddenly and, from somewhere in the house, a voice roared, 'Haven't I told you before . . . '

Leendert's face had disappeared too. Frank stared at the house, at the windows, the doors, the red stone walls and the green gutter. At the gravel in the yard and the wandering chickens. He looked as though he were memorizing everything he saw.

Suddenly they heard shuffling footsteps. The back door opened and the housekeeper looked out nervously, her finger on her lips. Her need for quiet seemed unnecessary, for a great deal of noise was coming from inside the house.

Krina gestured over her shoulder. 'Listen to that,' she said. 'There'll be fighting.'

'It doesn't matter,' said Andreas angrily. 'He's taken Antoine.'

'I'll let him out,' Krina whispered, a little more calmly. 'But I don't want the police in the house. It never happened when his wife was alive. And it won't happen now. Not while I'm here.'

The boys were curious. Why was she so afraid of the police? Andreas put their thoughts into words.

'Haven't you heard?' the old woman whispered.

The boys moved towards her, jostling each other in the gloom. 'We'll go away if you tell us.'

The housekeeper looked nervously behind her. 'I thought everyone knew,' she said.

'Well, we know about the quarrel . . . ' Andreas began.

Krina said wearily, 'Oh, they're such fools . . . '

'Brakman?' said Frank.

'Yes,' said Krina. 'And his neighbour Slingeling.'

The boys held their breath. Slowly, in fits and starts, the story came.

'Neither of them will accept responsibility for cleaning the ditch that divides their land. Brakman's against everything, as you know. In the parish council and everywhere. "I don't hold with it," he always says. "But I'll do it if I'm forced." That's fool's talk, I told him. But he never listens. Anyway, the man from the Water Board came but they wouldn't listen to reason. Brakman wouldn't, and neither would Slingeling over there. Then the Water Board sent a bill for the cost of cleaning the ditch.' Krina covered her wrinkled face with her hands at the memory. 'He attacked the postman! It wasn't *his* fault, was it? And now everything's even worse. Brakman won't let anyone use the path, not even the little Poldermans. They used it because the lane is in such a terrible state. That's his fault too. The Water Board would repair the lane if only Brakman would pay his rates. But no. And now the children have been taken away from the school. Brakman and Slingeling say that Polderman should repair the lane himself. But Polderman's stood firm, too. It's a shame, he's in the right, it's not *his* fault. A working man with five children and another on the way. But now Miss Jonathan's gone and all because of those fools, those half-wits!'

Krina paused. She seemed much calmer now. Then she went on, 'Brakman gets carried away when he's angry. I expect he's regretting it now. But he can't change his mind. He's too obstinate for that. His father was the same, and his son is, too. Like peas in a pod.'

Suddenly a deafening noise sounded in the house. The door flew open and Antoine ran out, pursued by a man with a broom and a boy with a stick. Shouting furiously, the little group raced across the yard and into the darkness.

Andreas looked at Frank in alarm. 'Should we go and help Antoine, do you think? If Brakman catches him again . . . '

Frank shook his head. 'Brakman won't catch him now,' he said. 'Antoine can run faster than any of us. He'll be all right. I expect he'll make his way back to the old car. We said we'd all meet there.' He turned back to Krina.

She shrugged resignedly. She didn't bother to lower her voice now. 'Well, we may as well face it. There'll be fighting. And the police will come. Sergeant Pateyn said that he'd come out if there was any trouble.' Suddenly she began to cry.

The boys shuffled uneasily on the hard ground.

Andreas didn't understand how Sergeant Pateyn would know when to come.

'Mrs Polderman's already complained twice to him,' Krina said. 'And who can blame her?'

Andreas cleared his throat. 'What did Sergeant Pateyn say?' he asked.

'He said that the path and the lane were council matters and nothing to do with him,' Krina said harshly. 'But he'd be here the minute there was any violence. That's what he said. And it'll happen. Just wait and see.'

As she spoke a flock of wild geese rustled past over their heads. The air was suddenly filled with their mysterious squeaking and cackling. The sky was dark now but the white fields still shone. The tall trees on the dikes looked like sticks of charcoal.

Krina shook her head and went into the house. The door closed quietly behind her. The boys stood where they were, uncertain what to do next.

'Which of Polderman's children is on the way?' Andreas asked.

Frank didn't know. 'If you ask me, they're all on the way,' he said. 'Coming back from school. I expect that's what Krina meant. She's getting old, remember.' He paused, and then said deliberately, 'Well, at least we know now what the quarrel's all about. So, if Brakman and Slingeling end their quarrel, then each of them will pay half the Water Board rates and the Poldermans will be able to use the path again. Then the Water Board will repair the lane and the Polderman boys will be able to go to our school all the year round and so they'll come back to the school and then – Miss Jonathan can come back. That's right, isn't it?'

In the pale moonlight Andreas could see the excitement in Frank's eyes. He was gazing now towards Slingeling's farm.

'Yes, that's right,' Andreas said solemnly.

'Then we know what to do now,' said Frank.

The boys left Brakman's yard and jumped over the ditch into the lane. Under their feet the snow was melting, slowly but surely. They could just see the deep tractor ruts that lay beneath.

7. Francine and Old Pier

Francine and the Rosseel sisters had gone in the opposite direction down the lane, towards the road. They had felt quite cheerful to begin with. They tried to work out how long it would take to send five hundred postcards to Mr Polderman. And then they had a contest to see which of them could walk the greatest distance with her eyes shut.

It didn't take them long to reach the crossroads. They had decided to scatter there, Francine following the road to reach the other end of the lane while the sisters set off across the fields.

'We'll attract too much attention otherwise,' Francine had explained. But now, in the cold dusk, the idea seemed less appealing. They stood at the crossroads and looked at each other, undecided. The roads were deserted and, in the distance, they could see smoke trailing into the sky from the houses. Marie-Madeleine sniffed loudly.

And then a car approached from the direction of Klaaskinderkerke. The girls stepped back to the verge. The car glided slowly past them and, through the windows, they could see two shadowy figures in the back seat. They recognized one of the passengers immediately. They knew that dark coat with the fur collar.

'It's Miss Jonathan!' shouted Jeanne-Marie. 'I know it's her!'

The car was well past them now. Soon it had become a black dot in the distance. The three friends looked at each other in excitement. They hadn't seen Miss Jonathan since December, despite the fact that she only lived in the next village. Marie-Madeleine sniffed again, and Jeanne-Marie told her to stop it. Obediently, the younger sister produced a white handkerchief and blew her nose.

'I expect she's going to the other side of the river,' said Francine bitterly.

The others nodded. They seemed to be growing colder with every minute. And it was getting dark, too. One by one the stars appeared.

'Do you think she saw us?' Marie-Madeleine asked hopefully.

Jeanne-Marie shrugged. It seemed to her that they had lost Miss Jonathan for ever. 'They say that there's a great shortage of teachers further north,' she said.

Francine said sadly, 'Perhaps she's gone already. To Middelburg. Or even Amsterdam. We'd never get her back from there.'

'It's no good talking like this!' Marie-Madeleine

said shrilly. 'We must get her back *now*. There's nothing else for it . . . '

Suddenly Francine grabbed her elbow and pointed upwards. There, in the dark sky, a shooting star flashed above their heads. The shining trail hovered over Klaaskinderkerke. Francine muttered to herself. And the others muttered too. Then they looked at each other in silence. Everyone knows that you should make a wish when you see a shooting star. Now, each of them knew what to do.

In a hushed voice, Francine said, 'Come on then. Scatter!'

And, almost solemnly, they walked away into the dusk.

Francine decided to go straight to her own house. I'll ask Jane, she thought. Jane helped on the farm and knew everything that happened in the village. Surely she would know who had started the quarrel.

When Francine arrived home, she didn't go into the kitchen for she could see that Aunt Lavinia had come to call. Whenever she came to their house, Aunt Lavinia always said, 'Shall I take your little brother away with me? Shall I?' and then laughed in a silly, high-pitched way. Even Sara never bothered to answer that question. Grown-ups could be remarkably stupid at times.

Instead, Francine went into the shed where Jane was milking the cows with the electric machine. It was warm and sheltered there, and the shed had a safe smell of animals and hay. The cows breathed heavily. One of them turned her head, gazed at Francine and then mooed loudly at her. Chickens scratched around at her feet. Jane finished milking and chased the cows back to their stalls. Their tails brushed across Francine's face as they passed.

'Jane!' she shouted. But Jane didn't hear her. Or pretended not to. Perhaps she was having one of her 'bad days'. You could never tell in advance when these would be, but they happened quite often. When they did, Jane would announce, 'I've got one of my bad days!' and stamp through the house and sheds, breaking things as she went. 'I just need to *touch* something and it breaks,' she would then explain gloomily. 'I only need to *look* at the porridge and it burns.' On those days she would slam doors and sometimes start to cry for no apparent reason. Father always grew very angry at this. He always said that Jane could pull herself together if she really wanted to. Mother was more patient. She always let Jane rant and rage until the mood passed. Francine hoped fervently that today was not one of the 'bad days'.

Jane carried a bucket over to the stall where the new-born calves were kept. Francine's own calf, Cara, was among them. She ran forward and helped Jane to hold the bucket of milk under their heads and guide their stupid mouths. A little bullock nudged her hands with his lumpy forehead. It didn't hurt but you could see that he would become a fierce bull one day.

Jane smiled at her across the bullock's back. I'll ask her now, Francine decided. She waited until Jane had cleaned the buckets and hung them on the wall with a deafening clunking noise.

'Jane, d'you know anything about the quarrel about the lane?' Francine said as casually as she could.

'Of courfe. Don't try and tell me you haven't heard about it too.'

Jane's voice sounded different. And then Francine realized why: three of Jane's teeth were missing. Mother had told her that Jane was going to the dentist the next day to have all the others taken out. This should have happened last Friday, but when the dentist had called her into his surgery, Jane had taken fright and rushed home. She had to go again the next day and so she was in no mood for gossip now. She checked the drinking water in the trough.

'Of courfe you've heard,' she said indistinctly. 'Everyone knowf about it. The Poldermanf are fweet people. But the otherf on the lane will quarrel with anybody given the chanfe.' She stumbled suddenly over the five cats who were clustered at her feet asking for milk.

Francine saw that she wouldn't have any success with Jane at the moment. It was all very well to wish upon a star. But would it make any difference?

'Did you fay fomefing?' Jane asked.

'No!' Francine snapped.

'Oh, I fought you did. Muft have been the wind, I fuppofe.'

Francine wandered out of the cowshed and into the yard. Through the open doors of the barn she could see two pairs of feet sticking out from under the enormous combine harvester. Her father and Gilles. Her mother was in the kitchen, cutting bread. Aunt Lavinia was probably in the sitting-room. Francine went into the kitchen. It was quiet there except for the rumble of the washing machine.

'Mother, d'you know who started the quarrel?' she said.

Her mother looked at her seriously. 'Now listen, Francine,' she said gently but firmly. 'There's no need to worry your head over that. Isaac talks a lot of nonsense. There's enough trouble in the world as it is.' She paused, and looked sharply at Francine. 'It's none of your business so don't interfere. Here.' She held out a thickly buttered crust.

The telephone rang, and Mother wiped her hands and went to answer it. Francine decided to go back to the lane and look about carefully until she found the quarrel. She would eat the crust on the way.

Outside, Ghislain and Sara were riding round and round on their bikes. Sara stopped when she saw

Francine and said, 'Where are you going? Can I come too?'

Francine looked doubtfully at the small red face. 'Come on, then,' she said, grateful now for the offer of company. She tucked Sara's scarf firmly into her collar and they went on their way. Ghislain watched them regretfully. He had no brothers or sisters. And his mother wouldn't be home from work until six o'clock. He decided to go inside and ask Sara's mother for a sandwich.

Francine walked on quickly, holding Sara's hand. When they had passed Wantje's shop, they crossed the road and entered the lane. They could see the lights of Brakman's house ahead of them, and other lights glimmered in the darkness further on.

Francine wondered where Andreas and the others were now. Perhaps he'd already discovered the quarrel. But how could you end a quarrel – especially if grown-ups were involved? Francine frowned. It had all seemed so simple in the daylight.

The snow on the lane was melting now. Before long the state of the lane would be as bad as it had been in the autumn when so much rain had fallen. And what would happen then? It was easy enough for grown-ups to end the quarrels of their children. But not so easy the other way round. Everyone had said that they should sort it out for themselves. Wantje had said this. And the teacher, too, according to Andreas. It wasn't as easy as all that.

A small hand squeezed her fingers. 'You're very quiet,' a voice said reproachfully.

'Sorry,' Francine said absently. 'What did you do at school today?' Her mother always asked that.

'We did sums,' Sara told her, as she had earlier told her mother. 'And then reading . . . '

'Ah,' said Francine, deep in thought.

They were now well into the lane and there, tucked away behind a little copse, lay the lonely house of Old Pier. He lived there quite alone with three fierce sheepdogs and a quantity of cats, chickens and rabbits. If you can call that living alone. Everyone said that Pier was a bit wrong in the head but people are always quick to say that about someone who doesn't do the washing on Monday or the dusting on Friday as they do. But Pier was a bit strange, all the same. He had been a shepherd once and for years he had wandered with his sheep on the dunes at low tide and on the dike when the sea was high. He always carried an accordion and he would play on it for hours, gazing at the sea as he did so. The dogs looked after the sheep and sometimes whined in time to the music. No one knew his real name; they had always called him Old Pier. Now he had become too old to manage the sheep and so he had retired to this little house. He was never seen in the village or on the roads or even in Wantje's shop. He looked after himself and obviously didn't need any help from anyone. People resented this, of course. 'Aren't we good enough for him?' they sneered. They said, too, that he threatened anyone who came near him with a gun, and that he had a treasure buried under the floor. He was a secret drinker, or so they claimed, and he never cleaned his house. The years on the dunes had gone to his head, and he stayed awake day and night in case anyone came near him. If he saw anyone, people said, he would set his sheepdogs on them. So it's not really surprising that Antoine should have warned the girls not to go near him.

Francine shivered. She gripped Sara's hand tightly and began to walk faster. Few people used the lane, only those who were forced to do so in order to reach the houses. Like the doctor. The children often went along it as it was more interesting than the dike road. And, of course, they used to come this way to play with the Polderman boys. Old Pier didn't mind children; he only really disliked grown-ups. All the same, neither he nor his dogs would allow the children near his house.

'Come on, we must hurry,' Francine whispered to Sara.

She decided that she would go and see Mrs Polderman. She wasn't a terribly friendly sort of person but everyone said that she wasn't as bad as some people they could name. After all, she had every reason to be bad-tempered, with a husband who worked so far away and five great red-haired sons to look after.

Suddenly, there was the sound of footsteps in the darkness. Someone had come up behind them. Terrified, Francine looked round to find Jeanne-Marie staring at her anxiously.

'Have you found the quarrel?' Jeanne-Marie whispered. 'You're standing there as if – '

'No,' Francine answered curtly. 'And I haven't noticed you looking very hard.' She said this to try and hide her fright.

'No,' said Jeanne-Marie, looking round nervously.

Francine swallowed. 'It's not much fun, is it? Being alone,' she said.

'How do you mean?' asked Jeanne-Marie soberly.

'Oh, nothing,' said Francine.

Jeanne-Marie looked at her sharply. 'You do talk rubbish sometimes,' she said. 'Anyway, you're not alone. Come on, let's go.'

'I was only going to the Poldermans,' Francine confessed. Secretly, she was very relieved to be with her friend again. 'But I didn't like the idea much.'

'I wouldn't either,' said Jeanne-Marie, honest as always. 'I was going to see Mr Brakman. But I don't like Leendert. He always teases me. So I'm not going, after all.'

'Then let's all go to Mrs Polderman,' said Francine, pleased.

They looked at each other and at Sara. The lane was empty and the houses were silent. Nothing moved.

'Er – shall we run? Past Old Pier's house? Then we'll get there quicker,' said Francine.

'Yes, all right,' said Jeanne-Marie. 'It *would* be quicker.'

They were whispering, without knowing why. They joined hands.

'Let's go then,' said Francine softly.

But the girls did not reach the Poldermans' that evening. They had hardly run a few yards when they heard a strange growling noise. They stopped, their hearts thumping. What could it be? The dogs, perhaps. They waited in silence. Old Pier's legs were bad but he might be lying in wait for them with his rifle. Perhaps he had sent the dogs to find them. He wasn't to know that they weren't grown-ups, that only children were in the lane in the darkness.

'There's a stick over there.' Jeanne-Marie spoke so quietly that Francine could scarcely hear what she said. 'Stay here. I'll fetch it. Then at least we'll have something.'

She crept away. Francine gazed into the shadows behind them. And then, suddenly, her heart leaped into her mouth. Something had moved. One of the shadows. Jeanne-Marie seemed to be making a terrible noise as she splashed through the deep ruts to reach the stick. And then Francine saw Old Pier. He was standing in the shadow of a small barn, looking at her. Oh, why didn't Jeanne-Marie come back? What on earth had given her the idea to fetch that stick?

The shadow moved. With a sick feeling in her stomach, Francine saw that Pier had brought a dog with him. Would he set it on Jeanne-Marie?

Francine squeezed Sara so tightly that the little girl squeaked feebly. At the same time she screamed, 'Get away, Jeanne-Marie, get away!'

At that moment, Pier stepped out of the shadows. His dog growled fiercely. Francine could not move. Her legs felt like jelly. There was Old Pier. Pier, who never came out of his house. Who sat by his window all day, listening to the radio. He had been spying on them all the time from his yard.

Jeanne-Marie stood still by the ditch. She was breathing heavily.

'Children,' a gruff voice mumbled. 'It's only children. Girls.' Pier stepped closer. 'So, what do you think you're up to here in the middle of the night. Eh?'

'Er ... Pier ... ' Francine began. She called him 'Pier' as if she had known him all her life. But she had never met him before.

'We weren't doing anything. We were only walking past,' Jeanne-Marie stammered.

'So why didn't you walk past? I saw you messing

about in front of my house,' the old man growled. His dog strained at the leash, obviously anxious to leap at their throats.

'We wouldn't dare to mess about.' Francine was trembling now. 'We know about the dogs . . . '

'You can trust animals. Which is more than can be said for people,' Pier snarled. He bent down and stroked the terrifying animal so softly and tenderly that the girls could hardly believe their eyes. Sara peered from behind Francine's skirt and stretched out her hand. The dog sat down at Pier's feet, calm and relaxed.

The old man stared at the children and then said, 'But *you* were messing about. Shouting.' He pointed at Francine with his stick.

Francine's cheeks burned. 'I had to scream,' she said stiffly. 'I thought you were going to set the dog on her.'

'Do you really think that I would have set the dog loose?' Pier asked grimly. And when the girls shuffled and coughed in reply, he went on slowly, 'Yes. Of course that's what you think. And why should you think any different?' He threw his stick on to the ground. They saw now that it was not a stick but a rifle.

Sara saw it too. 'Why have you got a gun?' she asked. 'Is there a dangerous enemy round here?'

Francine wished she were a thousand miles away. Sara was always the same. She always looked so innocent when she came out with her most embarrassing questions.

Pier turned towards her. 'No one's ever asked me that before,' he said in quite an ordinary voice. 'And I'll answer you, too. Come with me.'

He picked up the gun and led the children along a path and into the house. The girls followed him nervously. They had forgotten how late it was. And about the quarrel.

Never before had they been in such a strange house or seen such a remarkable room. A number of white chickens were scratching happily on the red tiled floor; large chunks of tree trunk were drying on top of the stove. Cats peered at the children with interest from a wooden crate and, in front of it, the biggest sheepdog lay protectively, his head on his paws. In a corner a goat lay completely at ease in a big box. He looked stupidly at the girls with his slanting yellow eyes and chewed hay quietly. A beautiful red accordion glittered on a chair near the radio. Pier put down his rifle but he did not take off his broad-brimmed hat. He chased chickens from three chairs which he then pulled forward for his guests. The chickens flapped angrily out of the door.

'So,' said Pier. He didn't seem very talkative but the three girls were no longer afraid. They watched Pier curiously as he crossed to a blue cupboard, opened it and took out a tin. It was a beautiful tin, black and gold.

Pier said, 'There should be some coffee left . . . ' He turned to the girls and stared at Sara.

Francine felt uneasy again. Was he angry with Sara because of her question? She said quickly, 'Sara's always saying stupid things . . . '

Pier looked at her. 'Stupid? Stupid?' he said gruffly. 'Tell me, who is the most stupid, the people who think I'm mad or a child who asks ordinary questions? Hey?' He burrowed in the cupboard again, and then went on grumpily, 'I know that I'm old and ugly and that everyone keeps out of my way. They think I'd set the dogs on them. They think I spy on them. Shall I tell you something?' He paused. 'Today is my birthday.'

The girls received this news with astonishment. Francine and Jeanne-Marie looked uneasily round the room. Birthday? But where were the cards and the birthday cake? There was nothing.

'How old are you?' Sara asked cheerfully.

'Seventy-nine, my lamb,' answered Pier. 'And I'll tell you why I want nothing to do with people. I've – '

At that moment they heard an enormous splash. Pier dropped the tin of coffee, picked up his gun, called the dogs, and rushed outside.

8. Andreas and Slingeling

Now that they had heard Krina's story of the quarrel, Andreas and Frank knew that they now had to tackle Brakman's neighbour, Slingeling. So, having left Brakman's yard, they turned up the lane and then ran confidently up the long, twisting drive that led to Slingeling's farm.

Slingeling was an unfriendly man at the best of times and the events of the past weeks had not improved his manner. He particularly disliked children. They damaged his ditches and paths, and then the Water Board, whose zeal for good order seemed so excessive, expected him to repair them. He saw the boys coming but, when they stopped by the conveyor belt on which he was sorting potatoes, he pretended not to see them. Perhaps they'd go away by themselves. But, after a few minutes, the boys' coughing and shuffling began to get on his nerves.

'And what do *you* want?' he growled. 'I'm not blind, you know.'

'No, sir,' said Frank politely.

'We were just passing and we thought we'd call in,' explained Andreas.

Slingeling looked at them suspiciously, and Frank nudged Andreas to warn him not to go too far. It wouldn't do to antagonize Slingeling. After all, they were trying to end a quarrel, not start another.

Slingeling turned back to his potatoes. The boys watched him nervously. It wasn't going to be as simple as they had thought. They couldn't stand there for ever. Then Andreas remembered that it was always polite to encourage people to talk about themselves. Everyone liked to do that.

'Is it a good crop this year?' he asked.

The farmer looked at him suspiciously. 'What's that to you?' he asked unexpectedly.

'I – I was just making conversation,' Andreas stammered. Slingeling's bad temper had unsettled him.

'You'd better go somewhere else if it's conversation you want,' said Slingeling. He turned the pages of a grubby notebook, and then licked a pencil and wrote something down.

The boys looked at each other desperately. At this rate Slingeling would have loaded his trailer with potatoes before they had made any progress at all.

'It's – it's beginning to thaw,' said Andreas.

'Oh no! Thawing! That's marvellous, that is. The lane and paths will be in a right mess before we know where we are. That's all I need. And – ' He stopped, annoyed with himself for talking like this to boys who were obviously up to no good. 'Well then,' he went on, 'what do you want?'

Andreas thought feverishly. His father always said that it was best to get straight to the point. 'We just want a bit more peace,' he said quickly.

The farmer's jaw dropped in amazement. And then he burst out laughing. His mouth was a black hole in his unshaven face. Frank stared at it, fascinated. Someone whose teeth were so brown should always keep his mouth closed. Quickly he lowered his gaze to the farmer's yellow clogs.

'Peace!' roared Slingeling. 'That's a joke, I must say. All you want is peace. I wouldn't mind a bit of peace myself. Now, out with it, what d'you really want? You can speak your mind to me.'

Andreas swallowed hard. 'We – er – well, about the quarrel . . . '

'*What?*' shouted Slingeling in amazement.

'Some people are quarrelling with each other,' Andreas went on cautiously.

'I'm not surprised,' said Slingeling. He thumped the sack in front of him. 'It's this fuss with the Water Board. And the snow. And ice. And now the thaw. It's enough to drive anyone mad.'

The boys nodded. Slingeling was being surprisingly co-operative. They moved closer, taking care, however, to keep a safe distance from the farmer.

'And it's beginning to thaw,' Frank said.

'You've already told me that.' The farmer was watching them with interest now.

Then Andreas said it. 'We've heard that you – er – that you've quarrelled with Mr Brakman about – about the ditch – and the lane – '

The explosion that followed could not have been greater if a grenade had fallen on the potato boxes. The farmer's face was twisted with rage as he screamed, 'What? You . . . I'll . . . I'll . . . ' He choked on his words. He grasped the trailer with both hands as if he wanted to pull it apart. After a

while he calmed down and said icily, 'Why don't you mind your own business?'

The boys were paralysed with fright. They wanted to run away but their feet seemed to be nailed to the ground by the farmer's furious gaze.

'We didn't mean any harm . . . ' stammered Frank.

Slingeling suddenly let go of the trailer and stamped round to where the boys were standing. They stared at him wide-eyed.

'And I thought you'd come for a few old boxes to make a rabbit hutch.' Slingeling raised his fists and shouted, 'Get off my land!' His voice was so loud that his wife came out of the house to see what was happening. 'Don't just stand there! Get out! Louts! Mind your own business! That's what I do and it's the best policy, believe me!'

Frank nodded, in spite of himself. His father often said that too.

'Quarrel!' the farmer repeated. 'The whole village knows that I told the Water Board the truth when they sent that bill . . . ' The memory fanned the farmer's rage again. 'Now get off my land!' he roared. '*They* sent you, didn't they?' He reached out and grabbed the collars of the retreating boys. 'It wouldn't surprise me if that teacher's at the bottom of it. That conceited little schoolmaster at Schellebelle! What does he think he's playing at? Sending children here. And it's always old

Slingeling who falls for it every time. I suppose he wants those Polderman boys back at the school. Well, I won't listen! I won't do it! D'you hear?'

They were near the gate now. Andreas and Frank looked at each other anxiously. Would he let them go? Or would he lock them up, as Antoine had been locked up by Brakman? They began to struggle.

'Miserable brats, that's what you are.' Slingeling released them angrily. And they ran.

They came to a stop in the lane, clutching their sides. Andreas' heart was pounding like a pneumatic drill and Frank's face was bright red. They didn't dare look at each other.

At last Andreas said in a strained voice, 'So we've done it again.'

'You and your bright ideas,' Frank said viciously.

They looked furiously at each other. Both felt miserable. They had achieved nothing despite all their efforts. In fact, they seemed to be making things worse. *And* they'd been called miserable brats.

'Well, I've had enough,' Frank said angrily. 'I'm fed up with – '

Andreas silenced him with a nudge. 'Look, what's that?'

Frank looked at his friend, who went to pick something up from the grassy verge. Something blue and white. Striped. Frank knew what it was.

He looked at Andreas in alarm. Their anger was forgotten now.

'It's Sara's cap,' Andreas said. His teeth were chattering. 'Frank, oh Frank, you don't think . . . '

Frank didn't dare answer. There were often stories in the papers about little children drowning in ditches. He looked hesitantly at Andreas who was twisting the woollen cap in his fingers. He suddenly seemed so desolate and miserable that Frank wanted to reach out to him. His gaze moved to the dark, gleaming ditch. It was very deep. And Andreas . . . His reaction seemed so unexpected. He always annoyed his sisters whenever he got the chance. But to see his face now . . .

'Cheer up!' Frank said. 'I'm sure it's not as bad . . . *hey!*' He bent down suddenly and said, 'Was she wearing boots or clogs?'

'Clogs, I think,' said Andreas. He stared at the ditch. And at Frank, who was peering closely at the waving grass. Frank stood up and began to walk in the direction of the house where Old Pier lived.

Andreas realized now what Frank was doing. He was pretending to have seen something. To reassure him. Only a fool would go anywhere near Old Pier. Certainly not Sara. No, there'd obviously been a terrible accident. If only he'd been there! Then it wouldn't have happened. How was he going to tell his mother? She relied on him to look after his sisters. He was close to tears now but he forced himself to look at Frank who was crawling like a Red Indian under the windows of Pier's house. He pulled himself up, listened at one of the windows and then beckoned to Andreas. Andreas crouched down reluctantly and joined Frank underneath the window. They raised their heads and peered through a chink in the yellow curtains. Then they dropped quickly down.

The friends looked at each other incredulously, and then Andreas whispered, 'I don't believe it! A man like *that* . . . '

He stood up. Frank pulled him down and Andreas struggled to get free again.

'You fool, do you want to spoil everything?' Frank panted.

'He's got a gun, hasn't he?' Andreas grunted. 'And he's wrong in the head. My sisters are in there. With those dogs. And his gun. I'll – '

Frank flung himself at Andreas. All their suppressed rage and bitterness seemed to erupt in the grim and foolish fight that followed. Andreas was short and sturdy, but strong, and Frank could not hold out for long against the sudden savagery of his friend. They rolled over the cold ground, away from the house. Then Andreas pulled away from Frank so abruptly that he lost his balance and fell into the ditch with a loud splash.

The door of the house flew open. A man and two dogs rushed outside and the shouting from the ditch was drowned by furious barking. Andreas was dragged from the water a little more roughly than was necessary and dumped on the bank. Then a strong hand grasped each of them by the collar and they were dragged by Old Pier through the yard and into the house. They were pushed into a warm room where, as if it were the most ordinary thing in the world, Francine, Jeanne-Marie and Sara were sitting. They didn't look at all frightened. On the contrary.

Sara said cheerfully, 'You'll get dry quickly in here, Andreas. It's Pier's birthday.'

The boys sat down in a daze. Andreas was panting heavily. Pier appeared with clothes over his arm. He walked a little stiffly, as if he'd swallowed a walking-stick. 'Put these on,' he said curtly, and turned round to make coffee.

Francine took the coffee grinder from his shaky hands. The smell of coffee was very reassuring. How strange it was to be sitting in the house that they had always looked at with suspicion, with the man who had always frightened them so much.

Andreas was shivering, but when he had warmed his hands round his cup and drunk some of the strong coffee, the colour came back into his cheeks. The dogs were lying quietly under the chairs but they didn't take their eyes away from the children.

'Well, then,' said Pier, who had been silent up till now. 'What have you two been up to?' He said this in such an ordinary, matter-of-fact sort of way that the boys found themselves telling him the whole story about the quarrel and the Poldermans and the school. Nothing they told him seemed to surprise Pier. And when Francine told him earnestly that she was looking for the quarrel too, he spat a long stream of tobacco juice on to the floor and said, 'Looking for a quarrel? They're easy enough to come by. In my time, I've – '

'How did you end quarrels? In your time?' asked Francine.

'We'd fight,' said Pier. 'Someone pulled a knife on me once. These things don't happen by themselves, of course.'

The children fell silent. Frank and Andreas thought about Antoine and how he would have enjoyed this conversation.

'We can't fight Slingeling,' Andreas said grumpily from the depths of the old coat that Pier had given him.

The old man didn't answer. He turned the knobs on his radio and listened attentively. His radio was nearly always switched on. None of the villagers knew whether he really listened to all the early morning programmes, the weather reports, the morning exercises, the schools programmes, the shipping forecasts and the time signals. Wantje had said once that Pier was so fond of accordion music that he didn't dare turn the radio off in case he missed some. When accordion music was being played, he would take up his own instrument and play too, sometimes the same tune and sometimes a different one. He would rock to and fro by his window, and no one knew what he was thinking then. Perhaps he didn't know himself. Now he tried Radio Luxembourg and then Radio Veronica. But neither of them seemed to please him and he switched the radio off with a grunt.

'Nothing,' he said and then, as if it followed logically, 'I don't want anything to do with this quarrel. It doesn't get you anywhere. I keep everyone at a safe distance.'

'Is that why you need the gun?' Sara asked with interest.

Pier stared at her intently. 'I'll tell you something,' he said. 'It's my birthday today. Seventy-nine years old. I want to stay *here*.' He pointed to the red tiled floor and the blue wooden walls. 'I want to be here when I'm eighty. That's why I keep them at a safe distance.' He looked fiercely at her from under his shaggy eyebrows. 'And I'll tell you this. As soon as they get to know you're seventy-nine, they put you in an old people's home. That won't happen to me. Over my dead body! Pier'll stay here till he dies.'

He stood up and poured more strong coffee into the children's cups. On Sara's cup was written, in gold letters, *For my dear Granny*. Sara felt very proud to be allowed to drink from it. The others gulped their coffee with pleasure, copying Pier. They felt perfectly at home. Pier no longer frightened them and neither did the dogs. No one else had ever taken coffee with Pier in his house. If only the others could see them now!

Pier sat stiffly in his chair by the window, with his black hat on his head and a stick in his hands. He'd seen plenty of quarrels in his time, he told them. Nothing surprised him any more. And no one need tell *him* how stupid Brakman and Slingeling could be. He'd known their grandfathers. If the children wanted the lane repaired then they'd have to do it themselves. They shouldn't expect too much from the grown-ups. He knew what he was talking about.

Pier went on to tell them funny stories about the old days in Schellebelle. The children laughed and laughed until they sat limply on their chairs. And when at last, sucking bulls-eyes which Pier had given them, they clambered up the dike on their way home, they were laughing still.

Before he bolted the door behind them, Pier had said in his harsh voice, 'So remember, I won't go to an old people's home. And that's why I don't allow strangers on my land. But if you ever want to borrow the dogs . . . you never know when they might be useful . . . '

Then he had locked himself into his fortress once

again. And, before they had even left the yard, the radio had been switched on and the seven o'clock news was booming over the dike.

'It's seven!' Jeanne-Marie had shouted in alarm. And they began to run.

Suddenly Francine stopped dead. 'It's funny,' she said. 'We've got no further with the quarrel. But all the same . . . ' She wasn't really sure what she meant to say.

Frank said, 'I haven't laughed so much for ages. Who would have thought that Old Pier . . . And all the so-called normal people kicked us off their land.'

'Has anyone ever said that Pier's nuts?' asked Andreas. They were running again now. 'It's just what people *think*, isn't it?'

'He's not as nuts as some people I could mention,' Frank said darkly.

Andreas realized then that he was still wearing Pier's old overcoat. He looked so extraordinary that the others began to laugh again. Sara joined in too as she always did, even when she didn't understand the joke. At last they calmed down again, though Frank was left with a bad attack of hiccups.

The children crossed into the St Helena Polder. Frank looked at Andreas who was walking beside him in his wonderful costume. It seemed strange to think that so much had happened since Andreas had stood at his desk, so obstinate and angry, earlier that day.

I'll never forget this evening, Frank thought. Not as long as I live. He thought regretfully of Marie-Madeleine, who had missed it all. And of Antoine.

'Come on!' he shouted suddenly. 'Let's find out what happened to Antoine!'

9. Marie-Madeleine and the Water Board

When Marie-Madeleine left Francine and Jeanne-Marie at the crossroads, she decided to go back to the lane. She wasn't really sure what she was supposed to do but, as the quarrel was all about the lane, it seemed a good place in which to work out how it had all started.

The lane was thawing now and deep ruts were coming into view. Marie-Madeleine looked at them anxiously. She missed her sister and Francine. Undecided, she gazed at the scattered houses which lay on the other side of the ditch. She was close now to Mr Brakman's farm. His son, Leendert, was pushing a wheelbarrow across the yard. When he saw her, he grinned, displaying a row of crumbling teeth.

Marie-Madeleine put her nose in the air and walked on nervously. She was glad that Jeanne-Marie and Francine weren't there to see how afraid she was. A girl who was scared of a grinning donkey like Leendert wouldn't be much help with ending the quarrel. Marie-Madeleine clenched her fists. She was now in front of the little house where the

Poldermans lived. The house actually belonged to Brakman, but Mr Polderman was allowed to live there because he had once worked for Brakman on the farm. But, now that all the farmers had machines of different kinds, there wasn't enough work for men like Mr Polderman. And, in any case, they were able to earn higher wages in the factories. Mr Polderman was working now on the new bridge that was being built over the River Schelde and he travelled there every week on a big bus. Because he did this, Mr Polderman saw nothing strange about taking his sons from the school at Schellebelle and making them travel by bus each day to the school at Klaaskinderkerke.

Marie-Madeleine took a deep breath and, remembering that it was always best to get difficult tasks over with quickly, trotted up to the Polderman house, knocked at the door, and shouted, 'Anyone at home?'

It was too late to turn back now. She would say that her mother had sent her to ask . . .

The door opened and a woman in a brown striped apron looked at her sourly. 'Yes? What d'you want now?' she asked in a hostile voice.

Marie-Madeleine retreated nervously but the woman grasped her roughly by the arm and pulled her inside.

'Oh, it's a girl,' she said, and her voice softened. 'Now then, what do you want?'

At that moment there came the sound of something falling heavily, and then a splash. The woman and the girl stood silent in the shadowy hall and peered out of the window that faced the lane. Mrs Polderman was still holding fast to Marie-Madeleine's arm. Someone had fallen off a motor bike. There was the sound of scraping metal, and muffled swearing, and then a dim figure climbed on to the bike again. The engine started and the bike weaved on down the lane. The sound of the engine grew fainter until it sounded like a bluebottle on a summer evening.

'Someone else fallen off,' Mrs Polderman observed gruffly. She opened a door and pushed Marie-Madeleine into a warm, cheerful room. A fat grey cat blinked at them from the floor.

'It happens all the time. Especially when it's raining.' Mrs Polderman pulled up a chair. 'And when *isn't* it raining here, I'd like to know.' She looked sharply at Marie-Madeleine whose face was still pale from the unexpected greeting. She could see that Mrs Polderman wouldn't take kindly to any feeble excuses. She bit her lip. Whatever happened, she mustn't cry.

Mrs Polderman patted a cushion, looked sharply at the girl, and then said sourly, 'I really must learn to control my temper. But it gets on your nerves, being here alone all day. And whenever I want to go out I have to use that disgraceful lane. I don't mind telling you, I've had more than I can take. Much more.'

Marie-Madeleine looked up shyly. Mrs Polderman looked so tired and lonely. She looked away again, quickly. On the table in front of her lay a basket of darning, a writing pad and a ballpoint pen. Near them lay a small well-thumbed dictionary. Mrs Polderman seemed to be in the middle of writing a letter. Marie-Madeleine thought about the chain letter, and about the five hundred postcards.

'I only came to ask . . . ' she began, and then stopped. Mrs Polderman looked at her. 'It's awful, isn't it? Having to travel all the time?' Marie-Madeleine said at last. Perhaps she could persuade Mrs Polderman to talk about getting the boys back to the school at Schellebelle.

But Mrs Polderman was thinking about her husband. 'Yes, it is,' she said slowly. 'But you have to do it when you've got five children to feed. It was different before we came here. We used to live in the north, you know. But I couldn't get used to the people up there. At least I was born here,' she added.

Rain was now beating against the windows. It was a comforting sound and Marie-Madeleine relaxed a little, proud that Mrs Polderman was talking to her as if she were grown-up.

'Yes, it makes a difference being born here,' Marie-Madeleine said wisely. 'But it's a long way all the same. On the bus.'

The woman shrugged. 'It is. And I'm left alone all day. But the money's so good, you see. And so we put up with it. Especially now that . . . ' She smiled secretly to herself. 'Well, especially now.'

'Is it a long journey?' Marie-Madeleine asked curiously. She enjoyed riding in buses when they went on trips from the school. But it might not be the same if you had to do it every day.

'Oh, *hours*. But he quite enjoys it. The men all get on well together. We all go to meet him on Fridays and then we have a meal together. It's the best time of the week and that's a fact.'

Marie-Madeleine decided to mention the boys. 'If only Wolfert and the others could use the lane . . .' she began.

'Don't mention that lane to me!' said Mrs Polderman fiercely. 'You've no idea what we've had to put up with.'

Marie-Madeleine wanted to say that she had more idea than Mrs Polderman might think. But she decided against it.

'Now that you're here,' Mrs Polderman went on, 'you may as well know that I've been writing a letter. To the Water Board.' She pushed the writing pad towards Marie-Madeleine. 'It's difficult to concentrate when you're always being disturbed . . .'

She did not finish the sentence but Marie-Madeleine knew that this was her way of apologizing for her inhospitable welcome.

'This is a copy of a letter I wrote a month ago,' Mrs Polderman said bitterly. 'Go on, read it.'

And Marie-Madeleine read:

Dear Sir,

I hope you will be able to help me. There is a lane here that we have to use a lot but no one does anything about it. Last week I fell off my bicycle again with my baskets. Now I want to ask if the Water Board can do anything about it. At the moment it is so bad that it takes a long time to get along it. Isaac the postman says that it is the worst lane he has ever seen. If it did not rain it would not be so bad. Our boys cannot go that way to school any more because they get all muddy and dirty. Some of the farmers make deep tracks which fill up with water so that mud gets everywhere. If you could fill up the tracks then it would be better.

Thanking you in anticipation,

Yours truly,

Mrs Elisabeth Polderman

When Marie-Madeleine had finished, Mrs Polderman said bitterly, 'That's what I wrote. But d'you think I had a reply? Not a bit of it. So I'm trying to write a better letter. Perhaps the grammar was wrong in the first one. You never can tell, can you? Perhaps that's why they didn't answer. But it's not the sort of thing I'm used to, you see. It takes time.'

Marie-Madeleine's shyness had been replaced by indignation. It wasn't right that Mrs Polderman

should be treated like that by the Water Board. They should be told how difficult it was for her. What did *they* know about living on the farms and in the villages? What did *they* know about the dikes and the polders and muddy lanes? She blew her nose loudly. 'Give me the pen,' she said. 'And tell me what to put.'

Mrs Polderman pulled her chair closer. 'Dear Sir,' she began. And Marie-Madeleine wrote, as neatly as she could:

Dear Sir,

I am writing again about the lane because our hardship is great and so is our cry for help, for it has begun to thaw. I am only a housewife but on Tuesday I put some old roof tiles on the lane to make it passable. But yesterday evening a tractor drove over them and all my work was in vain so I ask you not to ignore my letter.

Mr Brakman can use his own path to get to Schellebelle. If necessary, I will collect signatures from the people who have to use the lane, like the baker and the grocer and the coalman and the people on bicycles. The man from the insurance has to come along the lane to collect money. Some of the farmers could help to repair the lane and my eldest son can drive a tractor and could help on Saturdays. Then his father would let him and his brothers come back from that other school that I was not in favour of. So I hope that you can arrange something quickly. We all have to pay money to the Water Board and that is only fair but when there are lanes in bad repair then one wonders where the money is going. The lane is so bad now that a horse and cart could not manage it this morning.

This cry of distress comes to you with the sincere compliments and earnest expectations of

Mrs Elisabeth Polderman

Marie-Madeleine had thought of the last sentence herself. She sealed the envelope with satisfaction. She wondered how many other letters were being written in Schellebelle, and then of the postcards that she and Francine were going to write. Isaac the postman was in for a surprise. Marie-Madeleine knew, though, that he would pretend that nothing unusual had happened. Postmen have their own code of conduct, like doctors. She looked at the grey cat and listened to the rain on the windows.

'How about a nice cup of coffee?' said Mrs Polderman, and then, 'Listen, what's that?'

They lifted their heads and listened. A boy rushed past the window, pursued by a furious man who splashed heavily through the puddles in the lane. They could hear his angry voice: 'Wait till I get hold of you . . . you . . . you brat . . . come here, you little . . . '

Marie-Madeleine gazed wide-eyed at Mrs Polderman who shook her head grimly and said, 'There goes Brakman again. The blockhead. The fool. He can't keep the peace with anyone. You've seen it for yourself now.'

Marie-Madeleine listened. It was quiet outside once again. Only the distant complaint of the fog-horn could be heard now. And the ominous sound of ships' sirens from the Schelde. She shivered suddenly.

'I'll be glad when that new bridge is finished,' Mrs Polderman said to no one in particular.

Marie-Madeleine guessed that she was thinking about her husband. He was probably sitting in an uncomfortable shed waiting for the rain to pass. And waiting, too, for Friday to come.

'If only the rain would stop,' Mrs Polderman went on. She left the room and went into the kitchen. Marie-Madeleine could hear the rattling of cups. She stared into the fire. It was red and mysterious and friendly. Outside, the melancholy sirens drifted from the distant river.

Mrs Polderman came back carrying two cups of coffee. Marie-Madeleine took her cup and warmed her hands round it, copying Mrs Polderman. They smiled at each other.

'I always wanted to have a little girl,' Mrs Polderman said thoughtfully.

Marie-Madeleine started to make sympathetic noises but she thought suddenly of Mrs Polderman's five burly red-haired boys and said instead, 'Boys *can* be quite nice.'

Mrs Polderman laughed. 'Yes,' she said gratefully. 'You're right. They're good boys, all five.'

Her face now looked as soft and tender as that of Marie-Madeleine's own mother. The grey cat lifted its head, and then slept again. And so they sat together, the woman and the girl, waiting for the rain to stop. The letter to the Water Board lay on the table between them.

When Marie-Madeleine returned home, well satisfied with her visit to Mrs Polderman, the others were nowhere to be found. It was now quite dark and she knew that it must be well past six o'clock. She put her head round the kitchen door and said cheerfully, 'Hallo, Mother!'

Her mother looked up. The kitchen was filled with the smell of newly baked waffles. 'Where in heaven's name – ' she began.

Before she could finish the question, there came the sound of car doors slamming. Then the back door was flung open and a stocky, red-faced man came in, dragging Antoine by the ear. Antoine was red and furious; he was struggling to get free.

The man shouted, 'I don't care how big your farm is, I won't be ordered about by your son, understand?' Then he saw that only Marie-Madeleine and her mother were in the kitchen. He stammered a little as he said, 'Oh – er – I'm sorry. I thought Mr Rosseel was here.'

'No, he isn't,' Mrs Rosseel said icily. She lifted a waffle out of the iron and replaced it with fresh batter. Then she looked at Brakman with interest. Antoine had at last escaped from his grasp.

When Mrs Rosseel asked calmly what Antoine had done this time, Brakman roared, 'What has he done? Hooligans! I was clearing snow from my yard when I heard shouting. And what did I see? Your fine son dancing on my barbed wire. And that's not all, they were rude to my son. They're always getting at him and it's time it stopped, that's what I say.'

'And is that all?' Mrs Rosseel asked. Her face was a little red but she was still extremely calm. Marie-Madeleine watched them both with frightened eyes as she helped her mother with the waffles.

'All?' Brakman shouted angrily. 'Isn't that enough? But no, it's *not* all, if you really want to know. I grabbed him by the collar and shut him in my house. To cool off, that's why. The monkey. And what did he do ten minutes later? He broke out of the cupboard like a bullock and ran straight out of the door and up the lane! And there I was chasing him on my old legs!'

'You should have saved yourself the trouble,' Mrs Rosseel observed. She gazed deliberately at her bowl of batter.

'Oh yes? Oh yes?' Brakman was almost screaming with rage. 'But he hit my son! And I won't allow *that*! This boy, he's – he's a wild beast. But listen to this, before he ran off he said to me, "Why don't you pick a fight with Polderman? Then you could finish the quarrel for good and all. And then other people won't have to suffer." That's what he said!'

Brakman was now so excited that he had to sit down to recover. Mrs Rosseel passed the waffle-iron to Marie-Madeleine and turned to face him. 'He said *that*?' she asked.

'Yes, of course he did,' Brakman answered irritably. 'The hooligan! He's much bigger than my boy, too.' He looked critically at Antoine. 'No, well, perhaps Leendert *is* bigger. But that's got nothing to do with it. He cheeked me and then he cheeked my son. And then he broke out.' He turned quickly to Antoine, who jumped back in fright. Brakman waved his broad forefinger at him. 'And *you're* barking up the wrong tree, my friend.' He turned to Mrs Rosseel again. 'You know perfectly well that I've never quarrelled with Polderman. With Slingeling, yes! He's a hooligan too!'

Marie-Madeleine suddenly felt very sorry for this red-faced man who was working himself up into such a fury over nothing. It seemed that Mrs Rosseel was thinking the same thing.

'Yes, well, we've known each other a long time . . . ' she began. She didn't sound at all angry. 'Let me sort this matter out.'

'Well, all right,' Brakman said. 'I – er – I'd expected the boss to be here. But if you . . . '

At a sign from their mother, the two children left the kitchen. A few minutes later they heard her and Brakman talking quite calmly at the back door.

'Then I'll be going,' they heard him say. 'Give my regards to Jacques.'

There was the sound of an engine starting and then a car crunched out of the yard. And then everything was quiet again.

The children returned to the kitchen in silence. The waffles were ready. Mrs Rosseel looked at Antoine. She pushed her glasses on to her forehead.

'Antoine, what's all this about, now?' She looked at Marie-Madeleine too, as if she suspected her of being involved. Antoine didn't look at his mother. He watched a sleepy fly buzz across the kitchen.

'Antoine,' his mother repeated. 'Is it true what Mr Brakman told me?'

The fly came to a halt on the table. It began to rub its legs together.

'Yes, Mother.' Antoine stared at the fly, and went on, 'We were only playing, me and Andreas and Frank. And then he shut me up. After a while I broke out. That's all.'

Mrs Rosseel sighed. 'Why was Brakman so angry?'

Antoine mumbled sulkily, 'He thought that I wanted to scalp Leendert.'

'*What?*' said Mrs Rosseel in amazement.

Marie-Madeleine said quickly, 'Mother, you know that – '

'Quiet!' her mother said.

But Marie-Madeleine persisted. 'You gave him those cowboy books. He keeps them in the attic. They're all about scalping. But he doesn't really do it.'

Mrs Rosseel sat down. 'So, I see,' she said at last. 'Cowboys and Indians.' Her glasses dropped down on to her nose again. She coughed and then got up and began to wipe the stove. The children said nothing.

At last Mrs Rosseel turned round. 'I'll go and see Krina and explain,' she said. 'She must have a hard time of it with Brakman. And yet – well, he was a completely different man before his wife died.' She pulled her dark hair away from her eyes and continued firmly, 'I don't want to hear any more complaints about you, Antoine. Understand?'

'Yes, Mother,' said Antoine.

'And where on earth is Jeanne-Marie? It's almost seven o'clock.'

'Well,' Antoine began. He looked at Marie-Madeleine. What on earth could they say? 'I expect she's with Francine and the others,' he finished lamely.

'Well, we can't wait any longer for her,' his mother said irritably. 'Come and eat.'

They sat down at the table and began to eat waffles. Mrs Rosseel had covered them with butter and brown sugar.

'What exactly is a Water Board?' asked Marie-Madeleine with her mouth full.

As if he were in school, Antoine chanted, 'The Water Board maintains the roads and digs ditches. A constant watch is kept on the sea dikes so that any necessary action can be taken when the tide is high.'

His mother looked at him in astonishment and then burst out laughing. 'Have another waffle,' she said.

Marie-Madeleine sighed with pleasure. 'It's a pity the others aren't here,' she said.

And then, after a startled look at the clock, her mother said, 'Where *is* Jeanne-Marie? It's getting late.'

She got up and opened the back door. Antoine and Marie-Madeleine joined her there and they peered outside.

High on the dike five dark laughing figures were moving: four medium-sized ones and one very small one. As the little group came closer, they could hear that one of the figures had hiccups.

'That's Frank!' Antoine shouted. 'He's always getting hiccups. Even in school.' He cupped his hands over his mouth and roared, 'Waffles!'

Shouting and laughing, the five children raced at last into the Stellahoeve farmyard. And if Mrs Rosseel had not sent Andreas, Frank, Francine and Sara back home with two waffles each, they would be sitting in her kitchen still.

10. Frank has an idea

The days passed, and the weeks too. Neither the Society for the Eradication of Feuds nor the girls' postcard project made much progress. They all agreed, though, that something would be done about them soon.

Towards the end of January, when the snow and ice had disappeared, it began to rain. It rained for hours and hours and then it rained for days and days. The rain fell for a whole week, in short, malicious showers. Then February came. And still it rained.

If none of the rain had drained away then the water would certainly have covered the children's heads. At least, that's what they thought. They discussed it, huddled over their bikes on the way to school, picturing themselves sailing along the road

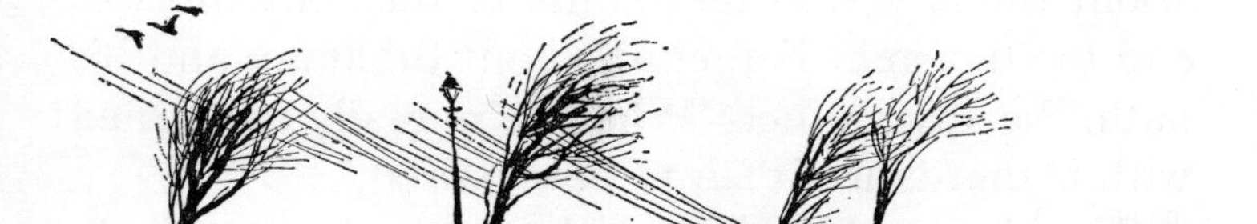

in boats. They had to shout at each other because of the noise of the wind and the distant droning of the Schelde. And, when they arrived home, they shouted still, and squabbled with each other. Their mothers grumbled about the dampness everywhere, and the smaller children were more difficult than usual. Few things get on one's nerves more quickly than rain.

The fathers had nothing to do. It happens like that on farms. For months they had worked from early in the morning until late at night, with no time to spare for their children. And now there was nothing to do but look after the cows and calves and clean the farm machinery. Such times are like a holiday for the farmer. And now the fathers of Schellebelle spent their days sitting sleepily in the kitchen or gossiping in the cowsheds. They took machines to pieces and then put them together again. Or they did nothing at all. And that is why Frank decided that it was time to give the fathers some work to do.

'Nothing's changed,' he said one day when Francine, for the umpteenth time, was chattering about the lane and the failure of their attempts to end the quarrel. 'Forget all about Brakman and his path,' he advised her. 'What we're really concerned with is that lane. It *has* to be repaired.'

'You know as well as I do that no one will do anything,' Andreas said sulkily. 'None of them will listen. They don't *want* to stop their quarrel. And it isn't even them who falls down on that lane each day. It's always someone else. And they won't even let us help sort it out.' He thought bitterly about his encounter with Slingeling and went on, 'So if you think I'm going to start on that all over again, then you're wrong.'

Frank ignored him. 'Nothing's changed,' he repeated. 'It's the lane that has to be sorted out. There must be an easy way to do it. Let's ask our fathers. They could repair the lane with stones and rubble. With their tractors.'

Andreas and Francine looked doubtful. They didn't share Frank's optimism. But Andreas could see that it was quite a good idea and said grandly, 'All right. They might not see it our way at first. But if we keep on at them, they'll come round sooner or later.' Andreas knew what he was talking about.

'Exactly,' Frank said solemnly. 'If you nag them for long enough, they'll always do what you want in the end.'

But it isn't always as easy as that, as the children discovered when they approached their fathers the next day.

'Look, Dad,' said Francine in a wheedling tone. 'You know that lane . . . the lane near the Poldermans . . . Well, it's always been bad but it's really *terrible* now. Don't you think you could . . . '

Her father looked up from the article he was reading about new developments in milking machinery. 'There are lots of bad lanes round here,' he said absently. He took his pipe out of his mouth and looked sharply at his daughter. He realized now what she was getting at. 'Now listen, Francine, just leave me alone. I've got the sugar beet to worry about . . . '

'Yes, Dad, I know,' Francine continued calmly. 'But we thought that you and the other fathers – '

'Why don't you just leave me in peace? Don't you think that would be a better idea?'

'Oh come on, Dad,' Francine persisted. Hadn't Frank told them to carry on until their fathers gave in?

'Later, perhaps. I'll see,' her father mumbled behind his paper.

'But there'll be no lane left at all soon,' Francine protested.

'The people down there can repair it themselves,' her father said irritably.

'But they *can't*!' Francine shouted. 'They can't move stones. But you can. You're strong.' Francine knew that men are susceptible to flattery.

' . . . the men . . . ' her father muttered.

'They're all quarrelling. And Mr Polderman is away most of the time.'

Her father became impatient. 'Oh, leave me alone, Francine. It's not my fault that Polderman goes away to work.' He frowned at his daughter and then said, more gently, 'Well, I'll think about it. All right?'

He pinched Francine's cheek affectionately, picked up his paper, and relit his pipe. Just then the door opened and Sara came in with a basket of kittens. They were barely three weeks old. She had found them in the barn and had immediately claimed them as her own. One of the kittens had something wrong with its eye and so she loved that one more than any of the others. She dragged the basket with her wherever she went, and even Jane didn't mind.

Sara put the kittens down next to the stove, close to her father's stockinged feet. He noticed nothing until the mother cat came into the room with a dead mouse in her mouth. When he saw her, he jumped up and shouted, 'What on earth! Sara, get these cats – '

'*Karel!*' Their mother's warning voice sounded from the passage.

Mr Almekinders muttered to himself and sat down again.

Francine decided to bring up the subject of the lane once more. 'Pier lives down there too. With his dogs and his goat and his chickens and his cats,' she said reproachfully. 'They might drown in the mud. You've got a tractor. If you could spare an hour or two, then – '

Her father slammed down his paper so suddenly that the mother cat looked up in alarm. 'And now I'll tell you what *you* can do for *me*! Write out a notice. A white notice. With big black letters that read "Do not disturb". And then I'll hang it round my neck for the rest of the winter. Understand?'

The paper flew up in front of his face again. He pushed his feet angrily in the direction of the cat basket, bumping the mother cat's head. The animal dug her long sharp claws into Father's foot.

He jumped to his feet with a roar. 'That's the last straw!' he shouted.

The children could see that he was really angry now. Sara dragged the cat basket away anxiously and Francine put on her coat and boots and wandered sulkily into the muddy yard. Andreas ran past her into the house, his eyes shining with excitement.

'Dad,' he shouted from the door and rushed to his father, bringing a cold draught with him. He prodded his father's knees. 'Dad, listen, we've got a plan,' he panted. 'You could help. If you and the other fathers . . . It wouldn't be too much work for you and – '

His father flung his paper to the floor and stood up threateningly. Andreas had never before been as frightened of him as he was now.

'Andreas,' his father said deliberately. 'I just want to say one thing. I don't want to hear that

lane mentioned in this house again. Understand? And shut that door!'

Andreas looked at him in dismay. All his excitement drained away. He looked round in bewilderment but saw only Sara who stood staring at him, the cat basket clutched in her arms.

Andreas dropped his arms to his sides. 'I didn't mention it,' he mumbled miserably. 'No one will do anything about the lane.'

'Nothing I can do will help,' his father said curtly. 'It's nothing to do with me. Let the council see to it.'

'It's nothing to do with the council,' Andreas said weakly. He felt unsure of himself now.

'The Water Board then,' his father said impatiently. 'It's none of my business.'

'If the lane was repaired,' Andreas said lifelessly, 'then the Polderman boys could use it to go to school. And then – '

'Andreas, it's not just a question of one little lane. There's more to it than that. And, for the last time, leave me alone. Now!'

Andreas swallowed. His enthusiasm had now deserted him entirely. He walked outside and splashed angrily through the puddles that gleamed in the yard.

'Now, Jeanne-Marie and Marie-Madeleine, I love you both but if I hear another word about that lane you'll have to spend the rest of the day in the loft.

D'you understand? Expecting me to repair that lane! Has all this rain gone to your heads? It's not my fault if other people neglect it. I've worked like a slave all year because I can't get labour any more. They'd rather work in the factories or on that new bridge. They earn more money and don't have to work as hard. *And* they have Saturdays off. When did *I* last have a Saturday off? They don't care about the land any more. And the ones who were born on farms are just as bad!'

The two sisters waited patiently for their father to calm down. Then Jeanne-Marie said stubbornly, 'But if the other fathers help too . . . Then Andreas says that the Poldermans – '

She should have kept quiet. Mr Rosseel turned round angrily. 'Oh yes?' he fumed. 'It's those Poldermans now, is it? They quarrel with everyone and *I'm* expected to do their work! In the middle of winter! I can't imagine what's got into your heads. So you think I'll heave stones about while *he* stands there watching me? Off you go, now.'

The girls looked at each other. Marie-Madeleine pulled on her white boots and Jeanne-Marie put on her red ones. Then they walked to the door.

'It's all right if you're cheeky, like Antoine,' Jeanne-Marie said loudly.

Mr Rosseel heard her, as she had hoped he would. But he grinned and said, 'Just you try it, my girl, and see what happens.'

Jeanne-Marie looked at him reproachfully. Mr Rosseel stared back at her calmly. He picked up his trumpet and began to play. He was a member of the village band.

His two daughters stalked angrily into the yard just as Antoine came into the kitchen, rubbing his hands.

'Father!' he said. 'D'you think you'll have any time to help with the lane – '

Mr Rosseel slammed down his trumpet and glared at his excited son. 'Has everyone gone mad?' he shouted. 'What's the matter with you all? Who in heaven's name has put these ideas into your heads? Hey? The teacher, I suppose. Wait till I see him . . . '

Antoine looked at him in astonishment. He had always thought that fathers put up with more from their daughters than they did from their sons. His father's violent reaction seemed to prove it. He frowned to himself.

His father picked up his trumpet again. 'The girls seem to have lost their senses too. I've never seen them like this before. And cheeky with it. Just tell me why *we* have to repair that lane? Why can't those layabouts down there do it themselves?' He seemed to be getting angrier every minute.

'They've had a row,' Antoine informed him unnecessarily.

'A row! The same old story! They've been rowing

for years. And I'm not surprised, either. I could tell you a thing or two about . . . ' He swallowed the rest of his sentence and went on, 'And so *I* must take my tractor down there, must I? They'd think I was out of my mind.' Mr Rosseel gestured at his head with the trumpet. Antoine began to laugh nervously. 'And now get out!' his father shouted. 'It's nothing to do with me! Sort it out yourself. But I'll tell you this, my boy, don't meddle in other people's affairs. No good ever comes of it.'

Antoine backed towards the door. He didn't want to turn his back on his father, for all the Rosseels had violent tempers and it was better to be safe than sorry.

Mr Rosseel looked at his son's stubborn face and at his dark angry eyes. Then, suddenly, he started to laugh. 'Your old wheelbarrow's still in the shed. You can make a start on the lane yourself. I might come and help you later. Next month.'

Chuckling at his joke, Mr Rosseel raised the trumpet to his lips. He didn't hear the back door slam. The silver notes of the trumpet rang through the house again. Mr Rosseel was practising.

Frank's father was standing next to the stove. He was a big, heavy man. In one hand he held a cigar and his riding whip, in the other he was holding a horse show programme. When Frank came into the room, his father was mumbling something about the possible winners. Mrs Camillemans was sitting at the kitchen table.

'If Baron doesn't win first prize, I'll eat my hat,' Mr Camillemans said, putting down the programme. 'He's by far the best in that class.' He noticed Frank standing by the door and said, 'What d'you want, lad?'

Frank cleared his throat nervously but his father didn't wait for an answer. 'It's almost certain that Gaby will be the national champion,' Mr Camillemans said excitedly. 'Everyone thinks so. You should see him. Three times reserve champion. Nine years old and a fine specimen, too. Did you say something, Frank?'

Frank said nothing. He wanted to say a great deal. He wanted to ask his father to help with the plan to repair the lane. He wanted to show the others that he, too, could persuade his father to get something done. It was his idea, after all.

'They're going to exhibit farm machinery this year,' his father went on. 'Like that new rotary harvester. And the D40L. That's got a new hydraulic system.' He waved his whip at Frank's mother. 'I'll tell you one thing, though. Those foals of old Grotepier's . . . '

She said in her slow voice, 'D'you mean the ones he sold to us?'

'No, no, no,' her husband said irritably. 'I'm talking about . . . '

With a sigh, Frank slipped from the kitchen. His mother noticed him go and called, 'Do you want some coffee, Frank?'

'He's a good boy,' Mr Camillemans sighed. 'But so quiet. It's a pity there's not more life in him. Susanna, about those foals . . . '

The 'good boy' did not respond to the offer of coffee. Outside, he pulled on his clogs and set off to the abandoned car, where they were all going to meet.

'What it comes down to is that they're all too mean to do anything,' said Antoine, when the children had reported on their progress. It was an unkind thing to say but they felt it to be the truth.

Outside the car the rain fell. It fell inside the car, too, for the roof had never been the same since a flock of cranes had rested on it in November. There seemed to be no end to the rain, and no end to their misery either. Everything they had tried had failed. The troublemakers had thrown them off their land. Their fathers wouldn't listen to them. No one wanted to help. No one. Only themselves. But they were only children. What could they do? They stared gloomily out of the windows. In books everything turned out all right in the end. But real life was different. They all realized this now.

'So, your father wouldn't help either?' Andreas said.

Antoine pulled a face. 'You should've heard what he said.'

'Just like mine,' Andreas said bitterly.

'And mine,' added Francine. Then she remembered that Andreas' father was her father too, and she put her hand over her mouth.

Frank did not mention his father. He mumbled gloomily to himself.

The children looked at each other uncertainly. Fathers always told their children not to quarrel, and to help other people, but when they tried to do just that, the fathers became angry. It was very odd.

Frank felt in his pockets. 'I'm going to buy some liquorice from Wantje,' he announced suddenly.

The others considered this a good idea, and they all set off. For once, the boys didn't complain about the girls coming with them. And when they arrived at the little shop, they even told the whole story to Wantje. Ever since Wantje had discussed Miss Jonathan with the girls, it seemed as though she half-belonged to their Society. It didn't seem to matter that she was seventy years older than they were.

'They're all mean,' Antoine told her heatedly. 'Too mean to do anything . . . '

'Just a minute, you,' said Wantje. She looked carefully at him over the top of her spectacles. 'Aren't you the little one from Stellahoeve? I carried your father in church when he was christened.'

They all burst out laughing. It was the first time they had laughed that day. Antoine was the only one who didn't. He went red, and clenched his fists. It was a ridiculous idea. His father was a big strong man who could play the trumpet. He wasn't a howling baby.

The girls were enchanted. 'Ah! How lovely! What did he look like, Wantje?'

Ever since the girls had first talked to Wantje about Miss Jonathan, they had been racking their brains in search of a plan to get her back. Jeanne-Marie had suggested that Miss Jonathan should marry the teacher. The school house was big enough for them both, after all. They enjoyed talking about weddings and wedding dresses. And about christening robes, which Wantje was discussing now as she pulled liquorice shoelaces from a drawer. But the plan for the teachers' wedding had come to nothing. It was Andreas who had gleefully announced that he had seen Miss Jonathan in Flushing, walking with a strange man. Arm in arm. This news had brought tears to Jeanne-Marie's eyes. Marie-Madeleine had stared silently at the ground.

As Wantje chattered on about the christening of Antoine's father, Marie-Madeleine thought about the teacher. He was so nice, with his black hair and dark eyes and slow smile. Everyone had laughed at their plan to marry him to Miss Jonathan. Everyone but Frank. He had noticed her sadness at Andreas' story about the strange man in Flushing and had told Andreas that he wasn't as funny as he seemed to think he was. Marie-Madeleine had smiled quickly at Frank then.

At last Wantje finished her story and the children moved noisily towards the door. Outside it was now dusk. Through a half-open door at the back of the shop they could see Wantje's husband sitting in front of a television set. He always watched from the time programmes began until close down.

Wantje called after them, 'It'll all turn out for the best, wait and see. And don't bother your fathers any more. I know them of old!'

Back in the abandoned car, Wantje's liquorice seemed to work wonders. No sooner had Frank put a piece in his mouth, than he said suddenly, 'I've got it!'

He pointed towards his father's farm. There, behind the house, stood an old barn. At least, it *used* to stand there. 'You remember the fire? When the old barn burned down?' he said.

The others nodded. As if they would ever forget!

'The funny thing is that it was all the fault of the Poldermans,' Frank grinned.

The others knew that perfectly well. Once, during the summer, the Polderman boys had dressed up as

Red Indians and lit a camp fire in a wigwam behind their house. The wigwam had caught fire, of course, but when one of the neighbours had told the story to Frank's mother, she had shrugged and said, 'Well, what do you expect? They've got to pass the time somehow.'

Frank had overheard this and made a mental note of it. He was often bored during the holidays, too. The next day, in his father's barn, he had set light to some sacks to see how quickly they would burn. They burned quickly and no harm would have been done if they hadn't set fire to the flax that was stored there.

It was Andreas' mother who first heard the strange popping noises. She'd thought that the sound was coming from people out hunting, even though the hare and partridge season had not begun. But then she had seen the smoke and realized that the curious noises were coming from the corrugated iron roof of the barn which was expanding with the heat of the fire. Frank's father had been out at the time but when he had been called home from the market and helped the fire brigade to empty the barn of machines, he had demanded a full explanation from his son. Even after all these months, the memory was still painful to Frank. He had only mentioned it now because it had come to him in a flash that the fire held the solution to their problem.

The ruins of the burned-out barn had not yet been removed. Frank pointed to them and the others listened breathlessly as he talked, their heads close to his. A few minutes later a triumphant shout rang out across the shining marshy countryside. Such a noise had not been heard there for months, not since the cranes had risen up with their strange cries and flown northwards in a wedge-shaped swarm. Now a flock of hungry crows, distracted from their search for worms, flapped angrily upwards. And old Gilles, who was carrying buckets of milk from the barn to the cowshed, pushed his cap back from his forehead and said, 'Look at that! Crows! A bad omen. And, what's more, it's Friday.' He shook his head sadly and went into the shed.

11. The tractor

'So I'll drive the tractor out of our new barn,' Frank explained. 'I'll go out of the yard, over the dam and down to the three willows. Then, when it's dusk . . . '

The others wouldn't let him finish.

'It's the most marvellous plan I've ever heard!' Antoine shouted. He was beside himself with pleasure. Something was going to happen at last!

Andreas nodded slowly, his eyes shining. The girls were silent with admiration.

Frank's plan was this. On Thursday evening they would repair the lane themselves, using the rubble that remained from the burned-out barn. This couldn't be done with wheelbarrows, of course. And not with their bare hands. Instead they would use the tractor that belonged to Frank's father. Frank often drove it even though he wasn't supposed to. But the boys decided not to worry too much about that. The important thing was that Frank knew how to drive the tractor.

Boys under sixteen aren't allowed to drive tractors, of course. They are forbidden to drive them along the roads or even in their own fields. But no one in Schellebelle worried too much about that and the local policeman, Sergeant Pateyn, turned a blind eye. He knew only too well that the farmers were finding it difficult to find labour because so many men were moving to the factories. A son could always help his father by driving a tractor on the farm. That very week, after school, Frank had helped with the laying of drainage pipes in the fields. He had driven the tractor back to the barn. And so it would be easy for him to drive it off in a different direction. No one would take any notice of him at that time of day. And there would be few people about to see him on Thursday because the local Farmers' Club was meeting that evening and most people from Schellebelle would be going. The children wouldn't, of course, and neither would Jane or Gilles for they had to milk the cows and see to the pigs and chickens and look after the small children. Ghislain would be spending the night at Sara's house. It seemed very unlikely that anyone would notice them at all.

In the days that followed, Antoine and Andreas and Frank became more and more excited, especially Frank. It would all be very difficult but it was important that it should be done properly. It was this that made the plan so exciting. He considered the plan from every angle, trying to take every possible flaw into account. Nothing could be left to chance. All the same, there was always the possibility that they might be seen, especially on top of the dike where there was no shelter of any kind. The boys knew that their fathers would be far from pleased to learn that their sons had driven a tractor on the public highway. And in the dark as well.

'We'll just have to take that risk,' Andreas said when the point was raised for the umpteenth time.

'It won't take long with the tractor, anyway,' said Antoine. 'And the meeting will last for hours.'

At last, Thursday came. For the mothers this was an ordinary morning and so they were bewildered by the small appetites of their children. Even the girls were unable to finish their breakfast.

'Perhaps it's because we're going out tonight,' the mothers said. 'But, all the same, it's very strange . . . ' But they didn't spend much time worrying about it because there was a lot to be done on the farms that day.

At school, the children could think of nothing but the evening to come. All the children in the school knew about the plan now, except the very youngest ones. During the days that had passed, piles of stones and rubble had been accumulated and hidden near the lane.

When the afternoon came, the children didn't know how they were going to endure the last few hours. They couldn't share the teacher's enthusiasm for fossils and for Charlemagne the Great. They had more important matters to think about.

The teacher was a little puzzled by their behaviour. He looked suspiciously round the class when Francine informed him that nine and nine were twenty-seven and observed sharply that even Sara could have done better than that. And his puzzlement grew when, after asking Antoine why he was grinning to himself in such a foolish manner, Antoine's astonished 'Me, sir? Nothing, sir!' provoked a flurry of nervous laughter from the class.

Marie-Madeleine felt a little ashamed, though she couldn't have explained why. She felt sure that the teacher could see from her face that something was going to happen. She gazed solidly at her desk all afternoon and didn't look at the teacher once. She wished that he could have shared their secret. But the boys had decided against telling him. Only last week he had given them all a stern warning about children driving tractors.

'It's obvious that we can't tell *him* about a special tractor plan,' Antoine had said firmly.

Marie-Madeleine had to agree with her brother. After all, the teacher came from the city and couldn't possibly understand how things were done in the country. It was just as well that he didn't know that even Francine could drive a tractor. Marie-Madeleine was pleased that Frank would be driving that evening. She trusted him. And he had said that she could be a look-out when he drove the tractor from his yard.

And then, at last, the time came. Nothing seemed ordinary in the dusk. The boys disappeared over the dike to take up their posts by the ammunition – as they called the piles of stones – and to give the other children their instructions. Francine and Jeanne-Marie stood ready by the willows beyond the dam.

Marie-Madeleine waited in the yard at Frank's farm and watched the village roofs grow darker against the sky. The trees on the dike looked like black cut-outs. Every now and then lights gleamed from the distant Schelde. She knew that these were warning lights on the coast but she still felt scared when they flashed across the dike.

There was a sudden sound near her. She jumped, and held her breath. Then a hushed voice said, 'Marie-Madeleine? It's me.'

'Frank!' she whispered with relief. 'I'm so glad you're here. It's . . . ' She wanted to say that it was creepy in the yard but instead she said, 'I haven't seen anyone. I watched all the time you were in the barn. But – '

They heard a sudden shrill scream and they both gasped in fright.

'What was that?' Marie-Madeleine squeaked. She was clutching Frank as if she would never let him go.

Frank swallowed hard and hoped that his voice wouldn't betray his own fear. He cleared his throat and said hoarsely, 'It's that miserable peacock of ours. They sound just like small children. I thought everyone knew that.'

The peacock screamed again. Marie-Madeleine didn't feel frightened now that she knew where the sound was coming from. She moved away from Frank.

'Come on, let's go,' said Frank in an ordinary voice. He patted her shoulder and climbed on to the tractor. There, in the dusk and under the stars, he felt like a general about to launch an important offensive. 'Here we go!' he muttered.

Marie-Madeleine too felt as though something very important was about to begin. Something that she would remember for the rest of her life.

'Just stay where you are until I've gone a fair distance,' Frank said. 'You never know . . . '

He took a deep breath. And then he started the engine.

A sudden roar broke the silence of the evening. Frank was startled by the noise. He had never realized before how loud diesel engines were. He settled in the driving seat, put the engine into gear, and edged the tractor forward. To Frank it felt like a heavy droning animal that, like his father's horses, would always obey him.

Marie-Madeleine ran forward and opened the gate. Frank drove through and she shut it behind him. He didn't look round again but peered nervously along the brick-paved road that ran in front of him. Now, over the dike. This was the most dangerous part. There was no protection here; he could only hope that no one would see him. He stared firmly in front of him as if by doing so he could avoid detection. And then he had reached the other side. It had worked!

The others were waiting at the bottom of the dike. The trailer had been loaded with rubble and now stood ready. Andreas had greased the wheels so that they wouldn't creak too much. No one spoke when the snorting tractor appeared on the dike. They watched Frank tensely until he stopped the tractor deftly in front of them.

Frank left the engine running and jumped down. 'I know it's noisy,' he said, 'but an engine that's always being switched on and off is more suspicious than one that's left running.' He seemed completely calm.

'You're right,' Andreas said and began to attach the trailer to the back of the tractor.

The boys now began to load the scattered heaps of stones on top of the rubble that was already in the trailer. As each pile was loaded, Frank edged the tractor forward to the next. There was nothing difficult about this for it was what he did when sacks of peas or onions or potatoes were being loaded in the fields. The others did not bother to hide their admiration at the ease with which he manœuvred the tractor.

They were all enjoying themselves. It was hard work, of course, but they were all sharing it and there were enough of them to get the job done quickly. Frank felt on top of the world.

They reached the lane and began to unload stones and rubble into the holes and ruts. When the first holes were filled, Frank edged the tractor a little further on. He noticed Marie-Madeleine standing beneath him. She seemed to be saying something but he couldn't hear her above the roar of the engine. He needed all his attention for steering now. It had begun to drizzle. He noticed that a large broken stone was lying in front of the front wheels. He put the engine into neutral, checked that the brake was on, and jumped down to pull the stone out of the way.

'Just to be on the safe side,' he mumbled to Andreas who came to help him. Frank noticed that a deep rut lay ahead of the tractor. He climbed on to the machine again and moved forward slowly. The tractor swayed and shuddered and then the big wheels turned and willow branches brushed past his head. He looked behind to make sure that he was steering straight. It was becoming difficult to see as the sky grew darker. The tractor plunged into another deep rut, the deepest so far.

'You're doing fine, Frank!' Marie-Madeleine called. 'We're nearly half way now. When we've filled this part we can start to unload the big stones.'

'Stand clear!' Frank said curtly. 'Tell Andreas I'm moving up to that big hole there.'

Frank looked at her like a general inspecting his troops. The tractor headlights gleamed on the dark puddles that lay in front. The lane was very narrow here. Frank estimated the distance between the back wheels of the tractor. One metre forty. One fifty perhaps. His hands tightened on the quivering steering wheel. The tractor lurched forward. Small stooping figures followed it.

They were now almost opposite the Poldermans' house. This was the worst part of the lane. The past weeks' rain had worsened the deep pits and ruts and, when one of the wheels stuck fast in a hole, Frank needed all his strength and skill to get the tractor moving again. A little further on, however, the tractor stuck fast in an enormous hole. The tractor pulled and jerked like an animal as Frank implored it to move. But the mud pulled too. Sweat streamed down Frank's face.

'Come on, come on,' he said aloud. 'Slowly, slowly, raise the clutch slowly . . . ' He did this, and

the snorting monster beneath him pulled and pulled . . . With a mighty jerk the tractor shot out of the hole. Frank looked back to see if the rear wheels were free and lost control of the steering wheel. Slowly, almost solemnly, the heavy tractor swerved towards a black gleaming mass of mud at the edge of the lane. With stately grace the tractor plunged into the bank and, very quietly, a small figure fell from the driving seat into the ditch. The tractor toppled over on top of him and lay roaring in the mud. The headlights lit up the entire front of the Polderman house.

The children would never forget that moment as long as they lived. They stood transfixed. They didn't notice the rain trickling down their faces.

Andreas came to his senses first. 'Switch that engine off!' he hissed. 'And the headlights. Come on then, help me.'

'He's dead!' Francine wailed. 'If only we'd – '

'Oh, shut up!' Antoine shouted.

Andreas had reached the dashboard of the tractor. He was crying as he switched off the engine.

There was a terrible silence. The children shivered with fear.

'We've got to get help,' Jeanne-Marie said. 'He could . . . he could be . . . '

They all knew what she meant. They were farm children, after all, and knew quite well what could happen when a tractor fell on top of a man. This wasn't the first time it had happened. None of them dared speak their thoughts aloud.

'Oh, quickly,' Francine moaned despairingly. 'Or else it'll be too late.'

And then it was Marie-Madeleine, the most timid of them all, who proved herself the bravest. 'Don't just stand there!' she shouted. 'We've got to make sure . . . ' Sobbing, she jumped into the ditch without noticing the mud and the water. Her white boots gleamed in the moonlight.

'Frank!' she shouted in a voice shrill with fear. 'Frank, listen . . . Frank, are you alive?'

The others caught their breath at her desperate cry. Francine stuffed her fists into her mouth to stifle her sobs.

And then they heard a slight noise. A muffled voice said, 'I . . . my leg's caught, I think . . . I . . . ' And then, more clearly, 'I'm alive. It's just my leg . . . Marie-Madeleine, can you hear me?'

'Yes, Frank, I can hear you,' Marie-Madeleine sobbed. 'He's *alive*!' she shouted to the others. 'He's alive! I heard his voice!'

They had all heard it. No one felt ashamed of their tears now. They had forgotten about the lane. The fathers would have to come. They were the only people who could help now.

'We've got to tell our fathers!' Francine shouted suddenly, and stumbled away into the darkness.

One by one lights went on in the small dark

houses and doors opened. People came outside: an old man with a stiff leg, a couple of boys with bright red hair, an old woman in a nightdress, a plump woman wearing a man's coat. They came and clustered round the children, whispering.

And the rain grew heavier.

12. Fighting in the night

Most of the people who lived near the lane had gathered in front of the Polderman house. They fussed busily round the children who stood in a mournful huddle by the tractor, looking anxiously towards the road. Seagulls flew overhead, their hoarse cries echoing ominously over the countryside.

And then, in the distance, came the droning of many cars. Faint flashes of light shone through the trees and then, at last, yellow headlights sprang into view on the edge of the dike. The cars turned into the lane one by one, and came to a halt near the children. Dark figures sprang out, doors slammed.

The children edged away into the gloom. Their ears burned with the angry, anxious words that were shouted at them. Instructions were given, someone rushed away. Then two figures rose from the ditch where Frank lay, his leg trapped by the tractor.

'Perhaps we can get him out by lifting that . . . ' That was the doctor's voice.

' . . . when the ambulance comes . . . ' someone else muttered.

'Should we move him before the police get here?'

Andreas bit his lip so fiercely that he tasted blood. How were they to have known that this would happen? Francine stood next to him, still panting from her run for help. He could see her eyes glistening in the moonlight. The noise and confusion in the lane were frightening. And the fact that they had caused it all made it even worse.

There was the sound of more roaring engines and Antoine looked up, startled. A tractor rumbled down from the dike. And another. The watching people moved aside, men helped to secure cables. A faint sound came from the ditch. Frank was saying something but Andreas couldn't make out the words.

'It's all right, son, quiet now,' a new voice said. It was Frank's father. He must have arrived in one of the cars. He was there by the ditch, a big heavy man. There was something reassuring about him. His broad arm was round Frank's shoulders now, beneath the mighty tractor.

The two tractors roared, drowning all other sounds. The cables stretched. With surprise Andreas saw that one of the drivers was Mr Brakman and the other his own father. Everyone waited. The children stared at the tractors with tear-filled eyes. They held their breath as Andreas' father turned in his seat to look back, just as Frank had done earlier. They hardly dared watch.

Snorting and grumbling, the tractors pulled, like angry monsters. There was a loud squelching noise, a splash. And, before they knew exactly what had happened, Mr Camillemans was holding his son in his arms and lifting him up to the lane.

Andreas shut his eyes quickly. He didn't want to see Frank's leg, the leg that had been trapped by the tractor. His own legs felt stiff and lifeless from the cold and rain but supposing one of *his* legs was gone, what . . . Frank's father brushed past him. Andreas dared not look up in case he should see that Frank's leg was crushed and bleeding. But he did look. Frank's leg was still there. It was hanging limply but it seemed to be in one piece. He could see Frank's face clearly now in the light of the many headlights. And he saw that Frank was smiling.

'Here's the ambulance,' someone said.

Broad white doors opened, a stretcher appeared and then, almost immediately, Frank's thin body disappeared inside. Marie-Madeleine waved hesitantly as Mr Camillemans got into the ambulance. The doors closed and the engine started.

And then the ambulance stuck fast in the lane. The wheels turned, the engine growled, mud spattered and splashed but the ambulance seemed to be sinking firmly into a mud-filled hole. The driver lowered his window and peered out anxiously.

The engine roared as he tried to move forward, and then backwards, but the vehicle was stuck fast. The driver switched off the engine and opened the door. The women were tut-tutting sadly but the driver ignored them. His sharp eyes had spotted Brakman's path which led from the lane across the fields. He climbed back into his seat and shouted to one of the men, 'If you can push me out, I can get through to the road along that path.'

He had spoken to Brakman himself who was still sitting on his tractor. 'It can't be done,' the farmer said gloomily. He seemed to have lost his usual belligerent manner.

The driver looked at him in amazement. 'Why not?' he snapped, and put the ambulance into gear.

Brakman said nothing but his face was strangely twisted.

A shrill voice shouted, 'Because he's blocked the path with barbed wire. *That's* why!'

The driver looked bewildered. The tension among the onlookers was making him nervous. 'Look, something's got to be done . . . ' he began angrily.

A woman began to cry. And it seemed as if everyone had been waiting for this signal. Suddenly all their suppressed rage and worry came to the surface, rage against the fools who would not settle their quarrel, and worry about the accident.

'Look what's happened now!' a voice shouted. It

was Wantje. With her black shawl around her shoulders she looked like a lost crow.

'Just wait till *you* need to get to the hospital in a hurry,' Old Pier shouted at Slingeling.

No one seemed surprised to see Pier outside his house. The other men said nothing. Instead they shuffled forward slowly, threateningly. The children watched anxiously. It looked as though there would be a fight.

Above the muttering of the villagers rose the sneering voice of Leendert Brakman: 'It's nothing to do with us! It's the children's fault, they're always – '

'He sounds just like his father,' someone said scornfully. It was Slingeling. He looked slyly at Brakman who was still sitting dejectedly on his tractor. Andreas was beginning to feel sorry for him.

Slingeling went on, 'A man who chases children from his path and then blocks it with barbed wire isn't going to care two hoots if they have an accident.' Andreas held his breath as Slingeling shouted, 'He's against everything! He admits it too!'

'You – you – ' Brakman panted. He was choking with anger.

One or two of the men coughed menacingly. It was certainly true about the barbed wire. But they hadn't forgotten what Slingeling had done. He always said that he'd co-operate with anybody. Perhaps, as long as it didn't cost him anything. The villagers despised him for that but they knew, too, that they were all to blame for what had happened. So they said nothing.

Slingeling shouted, '*And* he's a councillor too!'

The crowd waited to see if Brakman would now defend himself but he said nothing. He put his head in his hands.

And then a boy pushed from the crowd and rushed at Slingeling like a small tornado.

'Antoine! Don't!' a girl's voice shouted.

But Antoine didn't care. All he could see was Brakman's dejected face and his mother's sad smile when she had said, 'He was a completely different man before his wife died . . . '

Antoine darted between the legs of the villagers and leaped at Slingeling. He battered the man's chest with his fists. Slingeling, taken by surprise, lost his balance and fell backwards into a puddle.

There was laughter then until Dirk Slingeling shouted, 'Keep your hands off my father!' and ran towards Antoine. Andreas rushed to Antoine's aid. Some of the men moved forward to separate the fighting boys. The old women raised their hands in horror, and the girls screamed.

When the teacher rounded the bend by the willows and came in sight of the lane, he stopped and blinked in amazement. From the dike, the crowd had seemed silent and dejected. But now they had separated into struggling groups. Or so it seemed.

Everyone seemed to be fighting. The crowd surged and swayed in the light of the headlights and the moon. Figures were wriggling between the dark wet trees and near the angular tractors. Shouts of rage and pain rose from the pushing and kicking crowd. The headlights of the clumsily parked cars and tractors beamed steadily over the scene. Behind the crowd, Mr Almekinders had pulled the ambulance to safety with his tractor, and no one noticed when, at last, it roared away over the dike.

Mr Brakman sat on his tractor, high and alone. His mouth was opening and closing but his words were lost in the noise of the fight. Then a new beam of light appeared and a shrill whistle sounded. Someone shouted, 'Police! You've had it now!'

Suddenly the fighting stopped and the noise too. Some people slipped quickly away into the darkness, others tidied their clothes.

'So. You're fighting now, I see,' Sergeant Pateyn said sternly. He looked at them all placidly, his thumbs tucked into his belt.

The people of Schellebelle had known Pateyn for years. He was their friend, and he ran the dramatic society that presented a play every winter in Klaaskinderkerke. He was always careful to warn people beforehand if he intended to arrest them or charge them. This didn't happen very often, but they respected him just the same.

Someone told him briefly what had happened.

The boys who had started the fight struggled in the grasp of two men. When Frank's name was mentioned, Antoine lunged forward and punched Dirk Slingeling in the face.

Pateyn walked threateningly towards him and said, 'So, you haven't finished yet I see. Ah, it's the little bantam from Stellahoeve.'

Antoine kicked the sergeant's boots angrily. 'That miserable . . . I'll get him . . . I'll . . . ' he shouted, beside himself with rage.

Even his sisters had never seen Antoine so angry before. But Pateyn was not frightened of quick-tempered boys. He said, 'I know all about this business with the barbed wire. Now, off home with you. Quickly!'

He looked sharply at Antoine and gave him a push. Antoine retreated sullenly into the gloom. But he didn't go home.

'So, Pateyn,' a woman shouted. 'You know all about it, do you?'

Pateyn coughed nervously.

'Of course he knows,' another woman said. It was Krina. 'He should be ashamed of himself,' she continued reproachfully. 'A strong man like him. Do you know what he said when everyone complained about the trouble here? He said it was a council matter and that he couldn't interfere. He'd only come if there was violence. Well, we've had *that* now, more's the pity.' She blew her nose loudly.

'That's the law,' Pateyn said curtly. 'I have to keep to the law.'

'So, if accidents happen, that's the law too?' Krina shouted indignantly. 'It's better to fight than sort out a stupid quarrel peacefully, I suppose. And someone's got to have an accident before you'll do anything. Is that it?' She wiped her eyes with the corner of her shawl.

'I've got to keep to the law. It was a council matter,' Pateyn repeated uneasily. He wasn't scared but he didn't quite know how to deal with weeping women. Then he received help from an unexpected source.

'Pateyn's right. He couldn't do anything,' a muffled voice said.

Everyone looked up in surprise. It was Brakman. His anger had completely disappeared and he sounded weary as he said, 'I went to the police myself when this – er – disagreement first started. And they said exactly the same thing. A council matter, they said. So I went to the council offices. But my path wasn't recorded as a right of way. So I went to the lawyer who had handled our affairs when my father bought this land. And he said that the land was made over to my father, lock, stock and barrel. And that the path is my private property.'

'You see?' Slingeling shouted in triumph. 'So it's *his* fault!'

Brakman ignored him. He went on, 'I didn't

think it right that I should have to pay all the rates for that ditch. And that's why I blocked the path. If I had to pay all the rates then other people shouldn't be able to use my path. One does stupid things sometimes. If I'd known that *this* would happen . . . ' He blew his nose. 'It's the last thing I wanted. That boy . . . I'm – I'm very upset about it, I don't mind telling you.' He blew his nose again and the villagers shuffled uncomfortably.

Slingeling shouted, 'He's only saying that now because he knows he might be kicked off the parish council.' He laughed harshly. 'D'you know what else he's done? He's sent me postcards! Me! The fool! He needn't think he can get round *me* with postcards!'

'You should be ashamed of yourself,' a woman said.

Everyone turned round. 'Bette!' someone said. 'Well I never!'

It was Mrs Polderman. Five boys with tousled red hair stood protectively behind her. No one dared laugh at Mrs Polderman's hastily buttoned old coat or at the threatening boys.

'*He* ploughed up the lane one night on purpose,' Mrs Polderman said, pointing at Slingeling. 'I couldn't sleep that night and I saw him. So he needn't be so self-righteous. And he's driven his tractor up and down the lane when there's been no call for it.'

'That's true,' Marie-Madeleine said.

'How do you know?' Jeanne-Marie asked her in surprise.

Suddenly Antoine, who had crept back into the crowd, punched Dirk Slingeling and they began to fight again. In the confusion, Marie-Madeleine was spared having to describe how sad and desolate Mrs Polderman had looked on the evening of her visit. It was just as well for Mrs Polderman wouldn't have liked strangers to hear about it.

When Pateyn had separated the boys, Mrs Polderman pulled her coat more closely round her and said softly, 'You should all be ashamed of yourselves. You all thought it was a great joke, Brakman's barricade and my boys being stopped from getting to school. None of you did anything about it. No one helped. Only these children. They were the only ones who cared.' Her voice became shriller. 'The children were trying to repair the lane because none of *you* would do anything about it. And now that boy was almost killed because . . . ' She covered her face with her hands and began to cry. 'You know as well as I do that the lane's dangerous,' she sobbed. 'Especially *here*. If I'd only known . . . '

The men shuffled uneasily in the mud.

Old Gilles shouted suddenly, 'It was true when I said there'd be bad luck. There was that dream of Isaac's wife and then those black crows – '

'Don't talk rubbish!' Wantje snapped at him. He gazed at her in astonishment as she hurried over to Mrs Polderman. 'Now come along, dear. You shouldn't be outside,' she said softly and, with infinite tenderness, put her arm round Mrs Polderman's shoulders and led her into the house.

The sergeant rubbed his chin thoughtfully. The men remained silent. Dirk Slingeling tried, for the last time, to defend his father: 'Those children shouldn't have meddled in it, anyway,' he sneered. 'It isn't their lane. It's the Water Board's. *They're* the people who're responsible.'

A sudden slap on the ear stunned him into silence. Even his father was too astonished to protest.

'Yes, *I* did that!' Krina said firmly. 'And not before time.'

Pateyn said angrily, 'This fighting must stop for once and for all. A fine way to carry on, I must say.' He looked sharply at the children. 'Now whose idea was it?' he asked. 'Driving a tractor under age. And on the public highway, too.'

The children said nothing and neither did the grown-ups. Everyone knew, including Pateyn, that this law was always being broken. But, even though he was their friend, he was still a policeman. So they kept silent. A ship's siren shattered the silence.

'It was my idea,' a girl's voice said. It was so unexpected that everyone turned round curiously. Even Pateyn.

'Well I never! It's Rosseel's youngest,' said old Gilles in amazement.

'We *had* to, hadn't we?' Marie-Madeleine said shakily. '*They* wouldn't do anything. No one would do anything. They laughed at us. And Slingeling said he'd ruin the lane for good and all with his plough. Mrs Polderman told me. And people are always falling off their bikes. And the Polderman boys . . . ' Suddenly she stopped. Now she would have to explain how the boys couldn't get to the school and so had been sent to the school at Klaaskinderkerke. And because the number of pupils had fallen, Miss Jonathan had been forced to leave. And how the school at Schellebelle wasn't as nice as it used to be, and how grumpy the teacher had become. She didn't want to say these things to the whole village so she fell silent.

Loud murmuring rose up around her and Marie-Madeleine began to feel alarmed. She thought about her mother and the warm kitchen at home. And about Frank in the ambulance. Suddenly she began to cry as if she would never stop, just as she had cried half an hour ago in the ditch by the fallen tractor. She covered her face with her hands.

'Now, now,' a gentle voice said. It was the teacher. He pushed through the crowd and put an arm protectively round Marie-Madeleine and the other round Andreas who was standing next to her, pale and cold.

'They must be mad to think they could do it on their own,' Slingeling muttered.

'And why should they do it on their own?' the teacher said loudly.

He gazed calmly at the faces in front of him. He was free to speak his mind. He didn't own the village shop or depend on any of the villagers for his livelihood. The children had to come to his school whether their fathers liked him or not.

'We've got our rights like anyone else,' Slingeling mumbled.

'And where have your rights got you?' the teacher demanded. 'All this fuss about the lane and your miserable ditch. Where has it got you? A boy was nearly killed tonight. You don't care as long as you have your rights!'

The teacher was really angry now. The children shivered. Didn't the teacher know that you couldn't say such things? Didn't he realize that people hated to hear the truth?

'I've just phoned the hospital,' the teacher went on. 'I almost forgot to tell you. Frank is better than expected. His leg will be in plaster but he'll be allowed home next week. He was lucky. It could have been a very different story.'

Someone in the crowd began to sob. One of the farmers cleared his throat and said, 'It's none of my business, of course, but the children . . . I'll be here tomorrow. With my tractor and one of my men.'

'So will I,' said Andreas' father.

'You can count on me.' That was Mr Rosseel.

'I'll be there.'

'And me.' The voices rose around the teacher as he beckoned the children towards him.

'It's a pity that you couldn't have trusted me a little more,' he said. 'I can drive a tractor, you know.' He turned round and walked quickly away into the darkness.

With a squeak, one of the windows in the Polderman house was flung open and an untidy head peered out. It was Mrs Polderman.

'It's gone too far! That poor teacher! The man's driving himself into an early grave and none of you care. He's got to teach all the children in the school. All at the same time, too! And this quarrel's nothing to do with him. It's a crying shame, that's what I say!'

The children could see Wolfert Polderman looking at them over his mother's shoulder. The window was slammed shut and, a little later, the light was switched off. Everyone was silent.

And then Wantje said solemnly, 'Miss Jonathan can come back now.'

'All right, all right, come along now,' the sergeant shouted. 'It's all over. Back home with you.' He began to nudge the old women towards their houses. 'Hullo, what's going on now?' he said, shining his torch across the fields. 'I don't believe it . . . '

He didn't finish his sentence but everyone could see what he meant. There, in the darkness, Brakman was busy in his field. Stumbling, he was trying to move the pile of barbed wire. Without saying a word, two of the men ran to help him. Together they dragged the barricade away.

It was now quite dark. The moon shone peacefully over the silent landscape. On the horizon, distant churches and windmills were etched against the dark sky.

Slowly, the crowd scattered and drifted towards the village. And three tractors droned back to their sheds.

13. Miss Jonathan comes back

Andreas couldn't sleep that night. Whenever he closed his eyes he saw again Frank's frail figure, high on the tractor. The thin black trees, the shining lane with its ruts and holes, faces distorted with worry. He got out of bed for a drink of water. A cockerel was awake in the yard and was crowing deafeningly in the dark.

Later, Andreas awoke with a start. He looked wildly round the room. Had something moved? Yes, near the window. There was a long thin figure there. Someone's in my room, Andreas thought feverishly. He rubbed his eyes. There was someone by the window. Was it a man? A boy, perhaps? Frank, with his broken leg? Andreas slid beneath the blankets and shut his eyes tightly. After a while he peered towards the window again. The figure was still there, swaying slightly. Andreas put his head under the sheet and tried to sleep. But he couldn't.

At last he shouted, 'Dad! Dad, there's someone in my room!'

His father came at once. 'Go to sleep, lad,' he said calmly. 'There's no one here. You're only dreaming. It'll soon be morning.' He rested his hand gently on his son's forehead. And Andreas slept.

When he awoke again it was morning. He looked quickly towards the window. His long socks were hanging over the back of a chair. Were they the figure he had seen during the night? Andreas rubbed his eyes uncertainly. It was early but he would get up, all the same.

At breakfast Ghislain asked him if there was news of Frank. Andreas stared out of the window towards the farm where Frank usually slept. But not now. He was in hospital. Andreas pushed his food aside, pulled on his coat and set off for school.

His thoughts began to clear in the morning air. When he got to school he'd –

'Andreas!'

He turned round and gazed along the dike behind him. Antoine was running towards him with a newspaper flapping in his hand. Andreas stopped and waited until Antoine caught up with him.

'I – I was reading the paper,' Antoine panted, 'and I saw . . . ' He paused for breath. 'I saw this.' He opened the paper and pointed with a grubby finger.

Andreas read the report aloud. He could manage the difficult words for grammar was one of his best subjects.

Thanks to the resourceful action of a group of pupils, the village school at Schellebelle will shortly have two teachers once again. The school roll had recently fallen but it is understood that the required minimum of thirty-one pupils has been reached again. This fact is remarkable at a time when the dwindling population in rural areas is tending to decrease the number of children attending village schools. Schellebelle has also been affected by the drift of population to the industrial centres. It is assumed that the recently dismissed schoolmistress will be reappointed in her previous capacity.

Antoine looked at him eagerly when Andreas had finished reading.

'I wonder how they heard,' Andreas said.

'Who knows?' said Antoine. 'But it's there in black and white. So it must be true. They wouldn't have said it otherwise.' His face was shining. He seemed to be his old self again after the past miserable weeks.

A moped buzzed past them along the dike. Smoke was curling from the chimneys of the houses along the lane. Further on stood the old, square school house, propped up by the school next to it.

'Come on, let's show the teacher,' Andreas said suddenly.

They ran on. When they reached the school house, they crowded on to the porch and tugged the old bell pull. It shot out of the wall and Antoine fell with it to the ground. At the same time, the door flew open abruptly and Andreas stumbled into the house. The boys scrambled to their feet, covered in confusion.

'Come in, come in,' the teacher said cheerfully. 'The more the merrier.'

'The paper,' Andreas began. 'It says in the paper . . . '

The teacher closed the door behind him and gazed at the broken bell pull which Antoine handed him nervously. He looked steadily at it as he said, 'Why didn't you come to me? Don't you trust me?'

The boys wanted to run away but it was too late now.

Andreas stared at the doormat and said, 'You said that we had to sort it out for ourselves.'

There was silence. Antoine began to count the tiles on the hall floor.

At last the teacher said, 'Yes. I did. So everything that happened last night is really my fault.'

'No, it isn't, sir. It really isn't!' Antoine said.

He looked despairingly at Andreas who said stiffly, 'No, sir. It was because you told us that children shouldn't drive tractors. We thought you wouldn't . . . '

He stopped abruptly, red with embarrassment. What on earth had given them the stupid idea of showing the paper to the teacher? How could they explain that they liked him? That he had only been kept out of their plan because he would have forbidden it? It wasn't easy to put these thoughts into words. And now the teacher would always think that they didn't trust him.

The teacher looked at them seriously and said, 'You know perfectly well that I wouldn't have allowed it.'

'Yes, sir,' the boys said together.

'But what you didn't know is that *I* would have driven the tractor,' he continued.

The boys blinked at him.

'I would most certainly have driven it,' the teacher repeated. 'But you weren't to know that. And so I'm responsible for what happened.'

He put down the bell pull and searched in his pockets for his pipe. It was empty, so he put it back again.

'I've read the paper,' he said. 'The style is dreadful, if you want my opinion. But if you want to know whether it's true or not then – ' – he looked quickly at his watch – ' – run along to the crossroads, while I have some breakfast.'

The boys rushed to the door but the teacher called them back.

'One more thing,' he said. 'If you should ever make any more plans which need the help of someone over sixteen years old then you know who to ask, don't you?' His voice was serious but there was a twinkle in his eye.

'Yes, *sir*!' Andreas and Antoine said. They felt

ashamed and yet, at the same time, a great burden seemed to have fallen from their shoulders.

'Off you go then,' the teacher said.

He pushed them out of the door, fixed the bell pull back in the wall, and then went into the kitchen for his breakfast.

Andreas and Antoine ran in silence to the bus stop. When they arrived there, Antoine panted at last, 'I'd bash anyone for him. *Anyone*.'

A note had arrived at the school house that morning. It read:

Dear Sir,

Just to let you know that Wolfert and Jan and Daniel and Cor and Adri are coming back to you without fail. I hear that you need five more. You can sleep soundly now.

Mr Polderman

The teacher had already slept soundly when the note came. But, when he had read it, he felt more awake than he had done for weeks. He sang so loudly as he shaved that Isaac the postman had to shout to make himself heard. The teacher had stuck his soapy face out of the window to listen.

'There'll be an extra one for you now!' Isaac had bellowed. 'A new little Polderman was born last night. Another boy!'

The postman had ridden away, eager to be the first to spread the news. The teacher had stayed at the window, soapy and happy. Then he burst out laughing and picked up his razor again. It was going to be a very special day. And he wanted to look his best.

Francine was spreading syrup on her bread and butter when her brother left the house. This time she let him leave without asking to go with him. She knew that he was upset and she couldn't easily forget the despair on his face when Frank was carried into the ambulance. Anyway, she and the Rosseel sisters had already arranged to go and see if the Poldermans would get on to the Klaaskinderkerke bus that morning.

'Now or never!' Francine had said mysteriously when she telephoned Jeanne-Marie earlier.

Jane had heard her, and said sharply, 'That phone costs money, you know. You live five minutes away from her and yet you ring each other up every five minutes.'

It was obviously going to be one of Jane's bad days. Her new dentures hadn't improved her temper either.

Francine had murmured mysteriously, 'Everything will be revealed!' before she had hung up.

Now, as she ate her bread and syrup, she felt remarkably calm and confident. Was it because Wantje had said, 'It'll all turn out for the best?' Or was it because the adventure was now behind them, and their parents knew everything?

Later, when the girls reached the crossroads, they decided to hide behind a tree. There seemed to be many more people about than there usually were in the morning. They blew into their hands and shuffled from one foot to the other. Who would have thought that waiting for a bus could be so exciting!

At last the bus came in sight. It came towards them, a green shape between the trees. A curtain was lifted in a house on the other side of the road. Two boys appeared, Andreas and Antoine. An old man and an old woman were standing a little further on, peering towards the bus. Old Pier and Wantje.

The bus drew up and stopped. A sigh drifted from the small group of villagers when they saw that the Polderman boys weren't there to get on the bus. They grinned shyly at each other, cleared their throats, and pretended that they were only there by chance.

'So, they're not going to the other school any more,' Francine observed. 'That's something anyway.'

Old Pier muttered, 'There we are, then,' and wandered back to his house. The green door closed behind him. A little later the radio was switched on and the news resounded over the lane. A request programme would follow, and then the morning exercises. It was obvious to everyone that Old Pier was his normal self again.

Everyone nodded and smiled knowingly at each other, and then another door opened. Five Poldermans appeared, led by Wolfert. He was carrying a big white bag, almost as large as a pillow case. Everyone gazed at it.

'Is it his birthday?' Marie-Madeleine whispered.

'If it is, then it must be a very special birthday,' hissed Jeanne-Marie. 'I've never seen such a big bag . . . '

'Don't stare,' Francine said sharply, more to herself than to the others.

More children had joined them now, for it was almost time for school. They coughed, and pretended not to see the Polderman boys. The grown-ups had started sweeping their paths or examining barn doors. One of the men was so preoccupied with the marching Poldermans that he accidentally let his pig out of her sty. She rushed madly across the road, successfully diverting everyone's attention. The Poldermans marched steadily towards the school, walking carefully over the newly-filled holes in the lane.

The teacher was waiting at the school door. He walked solemnly to meet the Polderman boys. And, in a loud voice, he said, 'Congratulations on your new brother, Wolfert. What's his name?'

'Arjaan,' answered Wolfert, red with pride. He opened his paper bag, then thought better of it and closed it again.

'Andreas Almekinders!' the teacher called. 'Count the children, will you?'

Andreas turned. All the children in the school were looking at him. He counted.

The young ones couldn't wait for him to finish. 'Thirty-one! He's counted thirty-one!' they chanted.

But Andreas wanted to make quite sure. He counted, frowned, and then counted again. Then he turned suddenly to the teacher who stood watching with his arms folded.

'There are only twenty-eight!' he shouted breathlessly. 'But I know who's missing. Ghislain and Sara. And Frank, of course.'

There was silence. Everyone thought: what's gone wrong now? But then the teacher said calmly, 'Frank will be back next week. And Ghislain and Sara will turn up sooner or later. Anyway, they're still on the register.' He looked at the bewildered faces of the children and went on, 'Andreas and Antoine, go into my house and phone Miss Jonathan. You know what you have to tell her.'

The two boys disappeared into the school house, bursting with pride and excitement. Outside, in the playground, the others waited.

The only thing that Ghislain and Sara had understood about the unforgettable evening in the lane was that Miss Jonathan could now come back to their school. As far as they were concerned, only one thing was now left to be done. *They* would go and fetch her. After all, she was *their* teacher and so it stood to reason that they should go and collect her. No one else need know. The other children were always far too busy to take much notice of them anyway.

They were so busy that morning that no one had seen the two small children disappear. It was easier than they had expected to slip out of the yard without anyone noticing.

Ghislain took with him a piece of sausage and two hunks of bread and butter, while Sara wore a satchel in which two of her kittens bounced up and down as she walked. When Ghislain found a coin on the road, they had no doubt at all about their journey. Everyone knew that finding a coin meant good luck. In high spirits they set off along the curved dike that led to Klaaskinderkerke.

The sun glowed through the wisps of mist and haze that covered the fields. In the distance, a shining white ship glittered on the Schelde. The children felt very happy. They stopped once or twice to eat bread and sausage and to drink from the jam jar of milk which Sara had brought with her for the kittens. They gave the kittens a drink, too, before moving on.

They talked about caterpillars as they walked. And about quarrels. Although they weren't too sure what the quarrel had been about, they knew that it seemed to be over now and that everyone was very pleased as a result.

'D'you think they'll quarrel again?' Sara asked Ghislain.

'I don't know. I expect so. Grown-ups are always quarrelling.'

Before long they reached Klaaskinderkerke.

'We're there,' said Sara briskly. 'And there's Miss Jonathan's house.'

And there it was, a red stone house with a yellow door and a blue roof. They had seen it before. They walked up to the door and rang the bell.

A girl opened the door. She was carrying a duster. 'What do you want?' she said when she saw the children.

'Our teacher,' said Sara impatiently.

The girl shrugged and said, 'There's more than one teacher in the world, you know.'

And then, behind her, a door opened and a familiar voice said, 'But who have we here? Why, Ghislain and Sara! Come in, my dears, come in.'

Soon the children found themselves in Miss Jonathan's sitting-room. The kittens purred on their laps, while Miss Jonathan asked question after question. It took at least a quarter of an hour to tell her everything. She had heard about the accident with the tractor but it took them a while to tell her about the quarrel because they weren't too sure what it had been about. They were only certain of one thing: Miss Jonathan could come back.

'The grown-ups said so,' Ghislain said, his voice trembling. Had they *really* said that? Perhaps he had only dreamed it. He began to worry about whether Miss Jonathan would come back with them. She might want to wait for the teacher to fetch her. Or the fathers and mothers. Or the mayor. You never could tell with grown-ups.

'It's eight o'clock already,' Sara observed.

She could tell the time but Ghislain couldn't. Nervously he rocked to and fro on the edge of his chair. Miss Jonathan had gone out of the room for a moment.

'We mustn't be late for school,' said Sara.

Perhaps they were late already. What would they do if Miss Jonathan couldn't come back with them? Ghislain looked anxiously at Sara. She was staring at the door. Ghislain followed her gaze and then, as if by magic, the door opened and Miss Jonathan came in. She was wearing her coat, the coat with black fur and silver buttons.

The children slid from their chairs, their fears of being late forgotten. They looked up at Miss Jonathan's friendly face and realized how much they had missed her.

She took their hands. 'Come on, off we go then,' she said. 'We'll give the kittens to the lady next door. She'll look after them for the day.'

And so they went, out of the village of Klaaskinderkerke and along the dike, past the scattered farms and the crooked willows on which delicate new leaves were budding. None of them spoke for fear of destroying the magic of the morning.

The chimneys of Schellebelle were now clearly visible ahead of them. Ghislain and Sara could hardly wait to see the faces of the other children when they arrived with Miss Jonathan. It would be a surprise for the teacher too. Ghislain hummed to himself.

A man on a moped rode past them and then stopped. 'You there!' he called. He looked closely at Sara and said, 'Yes, I thought it was you, with your turned-up nose. It was you who told me that you didn't know where the St Marguerite Polder was. And all the time it was under your nose. Were you trying to make a fool of me?'

Ghislain wrinkled his nose and Sara stared fixedly at the man. They said nothing. Miss Jonathan was with them now and it was she who answered, 'Not so fast now. Nobody round here calls it the St Marguerite Polder. We call it the Griete Polder for short. *That's* why the children didn't know where it was. And a very good morning to you!'

The man stared at her in bewilderment and then drove on. The sound of his engine died away in the distance.

Then Isaac the postman rode past them. He

almost fell off his bike as he turned round to gape at the three walkers. When he saw who they were he laughed and waved.

Far in the distance the white ship was now a small dot on the river. A man was walking in the fields; he had a basket on his shoulder and was carrying an axe.

'It's going to be a good day,' Ghislain murmured to himself.

In front of them a big bird flew suddenly from a tree and came to rest in a field. It looked like a bunch of blue feathers on two thin sticks.

'What did you say, Ghislain?' Miss Jonathan asked.

Ghislain didn't reply but thought instead how wonderful it was that Miss Jonathan was coming back. And how glad he was that Sara had come with him to fetch her. He could never have done it on his own. He tried again to picture how Andreas and the others would stare with astonishment when he and Sara arrived at the school with Miss Jonathan. They would be at school now. In the playground. Or they might have gone inside.

They had now reached the old forge. Nowadays the smith had more business with tractors and machines than with horses. But today he was busy shoeing a brown horse as they approached. His head was bent low over the horse's hoof and sparks flew from his hammer. He peered under the horse's stomach at the three walkers and then dropped his hammer in astonishment. He cursed under his breath. Sara and Ghislain laughed aloud. Miss Jonathan laughed too, but softly.

The last stretch of road ran past the café and the old sheep barn, and past the entrance to the lane where so much had happened the night before. The children began to hurry, dragging Miss Jonathan with them. They were near the school. Ghislain's legs were shaking with weariness and excitement.

'Here we are,' he said hoarsely. He held fast to Miss Jonathan's hand.

The road seemed to be suddenly filled with people. When Andreas and Antoine had reported that Miss Jonathan hadn't been at home when they telephoned, the people of Schellebelle had begun to wonder whether she had gone to another school after all. Everyone knew that there was a shortage of teachers. Who could tell where she was working now? The children and the grown-ups had stood and looked at each other in disappointment. Well, they must have been mad to think that Miss Jonathan would have sat about and waited for them to sort themselves out. But then someone had suddenly shouted, 'Look! There's Ghislain! With Sara surely! And Miss Jonathan!'

They had all stared up the road in amazement. People rushed out of their houses to look. A group of women stood by the school gate.

'I told them so!' Wantje said with satisfaction. 'A school has to have a lady teacher, I told them. Make sure you get her back, I said.' But she still looked as amazed as the other women and old men. The younger men were all at work. Only Mr Brakman stood watching from his yard.

'They've got Miss Jonathan! She's come back!' someone shouted.

Ghislain and Sara proudly led Miss Jonathan through the school gate. The teacher was waiting for them at the door. He stepped aside, bowed low and ushered her inside. The first class followed her in and then the third class. The second class didn't go in because there wasn't one.

Outside, the bigger children looked at each other and then at the teacher who had reappeared in the playground. No one spoke. They knew that Ghislain and Sara had spoiled the grand welcome they had planned. The teacher stroked his chin and looked at the children. There was a twinkle in his eye.

Then Antoine said, 'Did you see the faces of those two kids? Like cats who've got at the cream.'

Everyone laughed, and the fourth and fifth and sixth classes followed the teacher into the school. As he walked, Wolfert Polderman quickly counted the cakes in his paper bag. 'We'll have to cut one in half,' he muttered. The last child entered the school. And the door closed.

Out in the road the grown-ups started to drift towards their homes, laughing and murmuring. From Old Pier's house came the sound of a shipping forecast. It was coffee time.

'Look, all of you!' a harsh voice shouted.

Everyone turned. It was Mr Brakman. He was standing in his yard, rubbing his hands nervously. He coughed and then went on, 'Krina's just made coffee. I expect you've got a lot to do but there's more than enough if you . . . '

Only Wantje noticed the tension in his voice. She said briskly, 'I could really do with a cup. Very kind of you, I'm sure.'

And, one by one, the others followed her into Brakman's kitchen. A little later, Wantje popped out again to fetch Old Pier while Krina took two cups of coffee over to the school.

Slingeling had watched everything that happened from the entrance to his farm. But he didn't go and drink coffee with the others. He turned away and walked slowly back to his house.

Peace reigned in the top classroom. The children were sitting in their desks as they had done before the Christmas holidays. What a long time ago that seemed now.

Andreas said, 'Sir, can I . . . ' He stopped in confusion. What did he really want to ask? 'Clean the board?' he finished weakly.

The teacher looked at him calmly. There was nothing written on the blackboard. 'Clean the board if you must,' he said, then: 'Now, where were we in geography? Ah, Australia. Right. Wolfert Polderman, what are the principal products of Australia?'

'Wool, wheat, butter . . . ' It seemed as though Wolfert had never been away.

In the infant class, Miss Jonathan was walking between the desks. Her hat and coat were hanging once more on the hook next to the sink.

Ghislain waited until she was near his desk and then asked, 'Please, Miss, why doesn't the capital I have a dot?'

The other children stopped writing and looked up attentively.

'That's quite simple,' Miss Jonathan said. 'The little i has grown so tall that his head has become joined to his hat. And because he's so tall he's called the capital I. Do you understand?'

'Yes, Miss,' said Ghislain, satisfied.

Miss Jonathan was a little bewildered by the sigh of relief that rose from the class.

Ghislain smiled happily to himself and bent over his book. The coin he had found lay in front of him. After school he would buy Miss Jonathan some liquorice shoelaces from Wantje's shop.

The sound of singing came through the wall now, the teacher's strong voice rising above the others.

Sara lifted her head and listened. She smiled to herself.

On the other side of the wall Andreas sang and thought of Frank. The teacher had said that he would be back at school in a few days' time. Then Andreas would paint a tractor on Frank's plaster cast with his new poster paints. It would look a lot better than the usual collection of signatures. And when the plaster was taken off, they would keep it in the loft.

Andreas sighed. It was a sigh of happiness. Because everything was ordinary at school. And because the fathers were going to mend the lane. And, most of all, because Frank would soon be home.

He decided that, when New Year's Eve came round again, Frank would be the first to ring the bell in the tower of the church at Klaaskinderkerke. But there was plenty of time to think about that.